THE DAVID PATON STORY

David Paton

sonicbondpublishing.com

Sonicbond Publishing Limited
www.sonicbondpublishing.co.uk
Email: info@sonicbondpublishing.co.uk

First Published in the United Kingdom 2023
First Published in the United States 2023

British Library Cataloguing in Publication Data:
A Catalogue record for this book is available from the British Library

ISBN 978-1-78952-266-2

Typeset in ITC Garamond Std & ITC Avant Garde Gothic
Printed and bound in England

Graphic design and typesetting: Full Moon Media

THE DAVID PATON STORY

David Paton

sonicbondpublishing.com

Acknowledgments

I'd like to thank all the musicians I've worked with and collaborated with throughout my career, I've had a blast.

A special mention to Stuart Tosh, Ian Bairnson and the late Billy Lyall, who shared the dream.

And a very special mention to my wife Mary and my daughters Sarah and Katy, my dream family.

Southern Fried Festival, Perth Concert Hall, July 2012. (*Marc Marnie*)

Forewords

It was 1975 and I was aged ten when I first heard 'January' by Pilot blast out of my small transistor radio. The song would go on to dominate the Australian airwaves that year, climbing its way up the Australian charts to land at #1 where it would remain for eight weeks. The song and the band's music instantly connected with me and became a favorite of mine. The song's Beatles-que sounding arrangements, its hugely infectious melodies and that magic – no pun intended – voice courtesy of bassist and vocalist David Paton forever etched itself into my soul.

In Australia, the band quickly followed 'January' with another Australian hit, 'Magic', which peaked at #12 on our charts before slowly disappearing from our airwaves and public consciousness. Yet for David Paton, his life and career became busier than ever away from the spotlight, and for the next forty-five-plus years, he spent time playing bass for some of the biggest names in rock and pop, from The Alan Parsons Project to Kate Bush, and from Elton John to Jimmy Page, Rick Wakeman and many others.

And this is where this book comes in.

David shares his life journey from growing up in Edinburgh, Scotland, to joining an early incarnation of The Bay City Rollers on to the heights of mega pop stardom with Pilot and beyond in its aftermath. David shares the highs and the lows, the achievements and the disappointments and all in-between, telling his story with an honesty and genuine spirit of gratitude for the life he's led. The book is an enthralling read from start to finish, and David's story serves as a testament to someone who followed his dreams with an integrity and passion for the music; his comfort with the fame it brought underscores this integral element fully. Along the way, as is the case with life itself, the bad times were all part of the journey and a building of character, a process that has made David who he is today and always has been.

I have remained a faithful fan of Pilot but more so of David. I have the utmost respect for him as an artist and musician and fellow human being, having followed his career closely throughout the decades. Having been too young at Pilot's height of popularity and with the band having never graced our shores, it wasn't until 2007 when I eventually caught David performing his Pilot hits live in Australia as part of the Countdown Spectacular Tour. Several years later, I connected with David via the wonders of the internet and since then, I've been privileged to have interviewed him for various music magazines and to call him a friend. Enjoy the book!

Joe Matera, Melbourne, Australia, 2022.
www.joematera.com

The name David Paton doesn't conjure up images of Grammys, glitz, or gyrating hips. His face may never have appeared on the cover of *The Rolling Stone* and he hasn't headlined the half-time show at the Super Bowl. Yet David has left an indelible mark in the rock and pop world. Clearly one of the most respected, underrated and versatile musicians in the business, David Paton has been writing, singing and playing great music for over half a century.

Early on in his music career, David's talent as a songwriter was quite evident. His catchy pop hit songs 'Magic', 'January' and 'Just a Smile' propelled his band to the top of the charts. There were few bands soaring as high as Pilot in 1975.

Unfortunately, some crew changes, poor management, and the demand for the individual members as session players ultimately led to the band's grounding in 1977. But a legacy of hit singles, two charismatic tours and four remarkable albums proved that Pilot was not some fly-by-night teenybopper band. The band took their music seriously, and it showed.

As a singer, David is equally impressive. The appealing melodies and distinctive harmonies he displayed with Pilot complimented each other and commanded your complete attention. As David moved on to other bands, such as The Alan Parsons Project and Camel, his vocals continued to captivate the ear. While most people are familiar with his Project vocals, some of his more obscure vocal work is worth noting. His singing on 'Heroes' from Camel's 1982 album *Single Factor* are simply mesmerizing. Once they get in your head, the haunting melodies may never leave. His vocals on his own traditional Scottish albums bring out the best of his versatility and ability to write in a particular style and arrange pieces of music by the likes of Robert Burns and Sir Walter Scott.

As a player, whether in the studio or on the stage, David is up there with the best. His bass licks on Elton John's tunes, such as 'Nikita' and his live performances with Elton were simply brilliant. His classical guitar work with Rick Wakeman is equally as memorable. The list of artists he has worked with is long and diverse, ranging from the hard rock of Jimmy Page, to the progressive rock of Fish, to the traditional Scottish tunes of such artists as Phil Cunningham and Dick Gaughan.

When one sees David play live, one really sees what he is all about; straightforward, no-nonsense, passionate music! David is too modest about his accomplishments and the last person inclined to herald The Alan Parsons Project anthem of 'Let's Talk About Me'. So, if you want to know more about his accomplishments and current work, read this book to experience the *MAGIC* of David Paton!

Kirk Kiester
www.davidpaton.com

MAGIC The David Paton Story

Contents

My Early Life In Edinburgh

In The Beginning

Towards the end of the Second World War in 1944, my mother was working in the cloakroom of the Excelsior Ballroom in Niddry Street, near the corner of The Cowgate, Edinburgh. During her break, she would make her way up to the balcony and watch the dancers below. It was there that she spotted a cute-looking soldier who was out celebrating with a few of his army mates. Mum was really taken by him, and when the band leader announced a 'lady's excuse me', mum made her way downstairs to the dancefloor and asked the soldier to dance. That was how a match made in heaven began for my mum and dad. They married in January 1945. My sister Nina was born in November 1946, and I was born in October 1949.

Edinburgh was a very different place then compared to the city we know today. It was a time when kids would play out in the street for hours on end, with little risk from traffic which was banned from 4 pm until sunset. This was an era when trams were in everyday use throughout the city for work or pleasure trips, and nights out at the pictures or a dancehall were a weekly treat. It was during the 1950s that Edinburgh became renowned as a festival city. It was the start of the arts and music festival and the delights of the Military Tattoo.

In order to meet the housing shortage as the Second World War was coming to an end, the government announced a temporary housing programme in 1944. These temporary houses were known as prefabs and just over 150,000 of these were built in the UK, including about 4,000 in Edinburgh. Mum and dad moved into a prefab in Saughton Mains, Edinburgh, and that's where I was born, before moving to Restalrig Square in Leith when I was about two years old. I vaguely remember attending Leith Academy primary for a few months before the family moved to a new housing estate in The Inch, which is just a few miles from the centre of town. Although I have fragments of memories from Restalrig Square, my recollections from The Inch are far more comprehensive.

1957. Eight year old David

It wasn't that unusual for me to be seen riding around the Inch housing estate in Edinburgh on my bike at eight years old, dressed as a cowboy, complete with cap guns in my holsters, spurs and a cowboy hat. I thought all wee boys wanted to do that; in my mind, I was Roy Rogers. It was during one of my scouts around the neighbourhood that I was stopped by the local hooligans George Moran and his sidekick John Smith. George ordered me off my bike and cycled away with it. I was left with John, who was a little bit threatening and kept telling me to 'shut the fuck up' even though I wasn't saying anything. George returned after about ten minutes and told me to get on my bike and fuck off before he rammed my cap guns and cowboy hat up my arse. I avoided them as much as possible from then on; it appeared that George didn't want to be a cowboy. Neither did I after that experience; I lost that sense of innocence.

I tried being a Native American Indian for a while but only succeeded in firing an arrow through the front wheel of Barbara Stanton's bike, causing her to fly over the handlebars and scrape her hands and knees on the tarmac. The police were called and came to our house, 'but he's only eight years old' my parents protested. After that fright, I turned my attention to something a bit more realistic. My Dad had been in the army; in fact, I think all our Dads had been in the forces at that time. 'Best man gunner' was a game the kids liked to play. The gunner would lie on the grass and we'd run towards him. He'd pretend to shoot us and the one who died the most convincingly had a go at being the gunner. This was fun until I fell on a broken bottle which embedded itself in the palm of my hand. I was taken to hospital and had four stitches inserted very close to my wrist.

Soon after that, I developed a very painful ankle. Mum thought it was something to do with the spurs I had been wearing; she had to take me by piggyback up to the doctor because I couldn't walk. I was diagnosed with osteomyelitis, a chronic infection of the bone that can happen as a result of an infection in another part of the body. An ambulance was called to take me to the children's hospital. I was kept in there for four weeks and had three penicillin injections in my bottom each day. Without penicillin, it could have led to severe complications.

So, I guess I was quite accident-prone as a boy, although now that I have two grandsons, I've discovered that most eight-year-old boys are the same!

1960. My first obsession with music.

I picked up my first guitar when I was 11 years old. We were having a family vacation in San Sebastian, Spain, and by that, I mean a real 'family vacation'. My aunt, my cousins, my Granny and Pop, and even the boyfriend of my sister were there. I really don't know how such a large amount of people were coordinated, but I don't remember there being any problem. Maybe that was the way to do it back then. In fact, I remember my aunt and cousins joining us on a trip to Wuppertal in

Germany when I was five years old. We must have travelled to Dover and then by boat over the English Channel. Mum told me I took ill with chicken pox during that journey. We travelled all that way to visit my Dad's army pal, who had married a German girl.

The trip to Spain was very memorable. San Sebastian has more Michelin star restaurants per capita than any other city in Europe; it is also the centre for Basque cuisine and has beautiful, sparkling beaches and incredible architecture. During the last week of August, thousands of people gather in the town to enjoy the unique spectacle of the running of the bulls. I somehow managed to get caught up in this event and was swept down the main street along with the locals, who were all dressed in white with red neckerchiefs. We ran as we were chased by several angry, thundering bulls. I managed to dive into a doorway to avoid being trampled or gored.

The bulls and the crowds thundered by and the noise and commotion began to fade into the distance. It was then that I could hear the sound of a guitar being played. This moment made a big impression on me; it was a kind of awakening. After all the uproar, disorder and confusion came the tranquillity and peace of softly played guitar music. I moved from the doorway and followed the sound. I had only taken a few steps when I saw a boy roughly my age playing the guitar. He was sitting on a window sill and seemed to be completely in a world of his own. I walked towards him and sat on the pavement, watching and listening to this beautiful sound. He must have been aware of me and gave a quick glance in my direction as he concentrated on his playing. I still recall the smell of the *agua lavanda* cologne that the locals wore, the purple flowers on the Jacaranda trees and the heat of the sun on my back while I sat there enthralled by this wonderful guitar music. My senses were buzzing.

Eventually, someone shouted at the boy and he disappeared inside the house.

I made my way back to the hotel, still shaken by the experience of being chased by the bulls, but I couldn't get the boy playing the guitar out of my head. As we were having dinner, my mind was still going over the events I'd experienced during the day. I wasn't really aware of what was happening during the meal until my Aunt Francis offered me a sneaky wee sip of sweet wine to help bring me back down to earth.

From then on, I pestered my parents to buy me a Spanish guitar until they relented. We visited a guitar shop and my parents let me pick a guitar, just like the one I'd seen the boy playing. The smell of the wood and varnish, the feel of the neck, the sound of the strings being plucked and the shape of the guitar just fascinated me. To me, it was a perfect creation. To this day, guitars fascinate me; indeed, all stringed instruments do. They are works of art, show pieces that should grace every home. Every time I pick up my Spanish guitar, I'm reminded of that very first experience in San Sebastian. Of course, I couldn't play back then, but I just felt so drawn to this instrument I couldn't keep my eyes and hands off it. When the vacation came to an end, the guitar was placed in a cardboard box for the journey back to Edinburgh. Amazingly it emerged from the hold in the plane without a scratch. I sat for months learning how to play from 'Guitar for Beginners' books and any kind of music with guitar chords I could get my hands on. 'The Big Rock Candy Mountain', 'A Four-Legged Friend', and 'On Top of Old Smokey' were just a few of the titles I practised back then. I was just happy to play a song; it was a creative process that I felt I was in control of. I was learning and enjoying the process. This was what I didn't get from lessons at school. I was achieving results and at last, I'd found an interest in which I was passionate. The ability to learn and my enthusiasm for that learning all came together and it opened up a whole new world to me. All thanks to a guitar.

1960 to 1965. High school

I'd missed the first two weeks of my Liberton High School education because of our family vacation, so I was two weeks behind everyone and missed the class photo and initial enrolment.

The first day was a nightmare, I didn't know anyone, and I didn't know where to go or what to do, so I reported to the headmaster. In the 1960s, teachers were still wearing their graduation gowns in high schools; I didn't realise that until I came face to face with the headmaster. I presume that a well-dressed teacher was considered more knowledgeable, professional and better prepared, but personally, I preferred the relaxed, informal look, as it seemed much more friendly and less intimidating. He escorted me to the correct classroom and introduced me to the teacher, Mr Wiltshire, who was also wearing a gown. Mr Wiltshire pointed to an empty desk and I walked over to it and sat down. I was horrified to see George Moran and John Smith sitting there scowling at me. I couldn't understand what I had done wrong, but they made it clear that they didn't like me.

I didn't have much interest in schoolwork and my achievements were limited to a Cycling Proficiency Certificate presented to me in class like some kind of diploma. This only irritated the bully boys and they gave me a good thumping in the playground for being such a smart alec.

That's how I befriended Ian Doyle, my pal for many years and now married to Rose, who is the twin sister of my wife Mary. He was in the gang that roamed the playground looking for any smart alec that warranted a good kickin'. He liked my army belt and I liked his Boys Brigade belt, so we swapped and I was initiated into the gang. I can't believe that I went to school wearing an army belt and a donkey jacket which invariably had a skull and cross bones chalked on the back, a symbol to unify us, but Wee Louie, the metalwork teacher, didn't tolerate this aggressive dress code we had adopted. He lined us all up and made us wash it off in the boy's toilets before entering class.

Tough guys, eh?

Despite the outwardly aggressive look, I was a timid young boy. I didn't go looking for trouble and wouldn't thump anyone without good reason, except Ronald Nimmo, who mistakenly elbowed me in the face at a woodwork class and caused my nose to bleed. I chased after him when the final bell rang, followed by a few members of the gang. When I reached him and spun him round for a smack, I realised he was crying and I couldn't bring myself to hit him. Poor Ronald, he wouldn't hurt a fly and the elbow in the face was not intentional. I'm sorry for some of my past behaviour as a child and I'd like to apologise to Ronald now.

Like any young lad, I was involved in a few scrapes, but I only remember one fight. It was the last scrap I got goaded into and I didn't enjoy one second of it. It was a snowy winter evening and I was on my way to take part in some sledging with a few friends. Sledging took place on any street in The Inch housing estate that had a slight incline. As I walked along the road, I saw John Kline. I knew John; he lived just a few houses away. I had never had any grievance with him, and in fact, we were always quite friendly to each other. As I got within earshot, he started saying to his pals in a loud voice, 'Here comes Davie Paton; I can batter him'. It was an embarrassing moment, and I had to react. I walked toward him and asked him why he was saying that. He insisted that he could easily beat me in a fight. A crowd gathered. My friends were pushing me and telling me to thump him. His friends were pushing him as well until we finally made contact. I got the better of him quite fast. I remember my punches landing perfectly, and they were hurting him. It was over fairly quickly and he came off pretty bad. I had my gloves on and kept pounding his face until his friends pulled him away; he'd clearly had enough. The sledging didn't appeal to me after the fight, so feeling upset, I just went home. My Dad knew there was something wrong and I told him what had happened. He told me I'd done the right thing, but next time I should try to avoid an all-out fight. I vowed there and then that I never wanted to get involved in any more street fights. It was necessary to stand up for myself at a time when my reputation was at stake, but given the choice now, I would walk away.

I tried my hand at boxing for a while. I'd get the bus to the gym which was on the top floor of a building on Waterloo Place. I'd half run, half walk my way back home. It was a good five miles, but I always felt exhilarated after an hour of boxing. I'd walk from one lamp post to the next, then run to the next, repeating this until I got home. I'm sure many of us can relate to that. But after a few bouts, I soon realised that boxing wasn't for me. I didn't like being hit in the face and I had a bad habit of tucking my head down and not letting my opponent thump me on the nose, as I'd had enough of that from Ronald Nimmo.

Rugby was the sport I enjoyed and excelled at in school. I managed to do pretty well as a forward and always enjoyed the games on a Saturday morning. My art teacher was Roy Williamson, who formed the Corries folk duo with Ronnie Brown, and went on to write 'Flower of Scotland'. That song is more or less Scotland's national anthem, especially when it comes to rugby. I was delighted watching Scotland versus England on TV in 2007 and hearing them play 'Magic' back-to-back with 'Flower of Scotland'.

Roy never knew I played the guitar and my artwork was nothing to write home about, but he'd attend the games on a Saturday and I remember him cheering me on. I was happy that he at least knew me as a good rugby player. Sadly, Roy Williamson died of a brain tumour at a very young age.

Music became more and more important to me and I found myself sitting in at night playing my guitar while my friends were out looking for trouble. One Christmas present I received from Mum and Dad was a portable transistor radio. This was an amazing introduction to the great music coming from Radio Luxembourg. The station boasted the most powerful privately owned transmitter in the world (1,300 kW, broadcasting on medium wave). In the late 1930s and again in the 1950s and 1960s, it had large audiences in Britain and Ireland with its programmes of popular entertainment and was an important forerunner of pirate radio and modern commercial radio in the United Kingdom. Radio Luxembourg kept me up to date with all the current music and had a huge effect on my musical career.

Mr Kennaway was our music teacher; he was another one who liked to wear his graduation gown in class. He never really knew that I had any musical ability. Indeed, on one occasion, when, rather than sing in unison, I sang a harmony with the class – which was not what I was supposed to do – he stopped us and said that he heard someone singing out of tune. This was not what I expected him to say and it didn't do my self-esteem any good at all. As we continued with the singing lesson, I continued with the harmony. He stopped playing, stood up and faced the class and asked who was deliberately singing out of tune. He was looking in my direction. I was too shy to say it was me as I wasn't sure if he knew I was singing a harmony to the melody. My ear for music was developing quickly and I had all the enthusiasm I needed, but the only thing lacking was confidence. The best academic students at Liberton High School were the ones who were given guitar tuition and the riff-raff like me were dismissed as no-hopers.

Being a shy boy with very little confidence, I was the last one to stand up and say, 'listen to what I can do'. I'm still a bit like that today. It worries me now that there could still be other kids out there with a talent that is missed by their teachers. Perhaps it's less likely to happen now, but it certainly did to me. In the late 1990s, I received a letter from the headmistress of Liberton High School asking if I would attend the school on an open day. Apparently, my name was in a glass case in the assembly room, along with a list of my musical achievements. I wanted to explain to her that the school had not given me the help that I needed and in no way contributed to my success in music. But instead, I chose not to reply.

Meanwhile, I continued practising the guitar and received a lesson from a teacher at the Pete Seaton music shop in Newington, Edinburgh.

During the summer school break, the 'gang' would go camping. I was probably 14 years old by this time. The gang was George Moran (yes, good pals now), John Smith, Frank Skinner and Ian Doyle – there were always about five or six of us. Sometimes we would just get a tent and head off to Liberton Dams. But then we got more adventurous. We'd head off on an SMT bus to Birkenside, which is about ten miles south of Edinburgh. We had our own spot at the bottom of a field down by the river, accompanied by several curious cows. There was a little bridge which was perfect for jumping into the water from on a warm, sunny day. My Dad's tent slept six and everyone chipped in with pots and pans and provisions. It was during this time that I had my first experiences with the girls that would also visit the camp occasionally!

The Beatles

When the Beatles burst on the music scene in 1962, they had a huge effect on me and most of my friends. The local newsagent sold records and I was surprised to find two 45s featuring The Beatles. The records were 'Ain't She Sweet' and 'My Bonnie'. They're still in my record collection today. At the same time as discovering the records, I also found the Saturday afternoon BBC radio show called *Pop Go The Beatles*. I'd spend many Saturday afternoons in my room with my transistor radio tuned in to The Fab Four and being totally in awe of the music they were making.

I started to grow my hair in the Beatles style, but my parents were not happy. I got dragged to the barber by my dad, and he made me have a sensible haircut. I cried for days because I just wanted to be as much like a Beatle as possible. My parents realised that young guys were wearing their hair a bit longer, so they eased off on the way I wore my hair.

I met up with Eric Cloughley at school, who also wore his hair long and took a bit of stick for it with some of the other pupils. But it didn't seem to bother him too much and we became good friends. Cloughley is a strange name, difficult for some folk to pronounce or even remember, but it's pronounced 'Cloffly'. He said to me that the funniest attempt at his name was at the doctor's surgery when the nurse came into the waiting room and asked for 'Mr Couchley'. Eric was a very good guitar player and we started to meet at his house after school and run through the Beatles songs we wanted to play together. We discovered that playing the LP at 45rpm instead of 33rpm made the bass part much clearer. In that way, we could really focus on the bass and hear what Paul McCartney was playing. Their chord structures fascinated me. 'She Loves You' ends with a G6th chord, while 'All I've Gotta Do' begins with an E aug 11. This was taking pop music to a new level and it was great training for musicians like me. I don't think I'd have written 'Magic' without the Beatles' influence; I was absolutely obsessed with them. I could hardly contain myself when I got word of a new single or album release, or *The Beatles Monthly* appeared on the shelves at the local shop. I'd spend hours reading what they were up to and marvelling at the photos of them recording in Abbey Road.

In fact, throughout the early 60s, I was in musical heaven. Everything was happening and I was at a very influential age where everything musical was taken in and absorbed like a sponge. Neither Eric nor I could make our minds up if we wanted to play guitar or bass, so we ended up sharing. That was really ideal for both of us. We'd play for hours and learn a lot together. This was great ear training for us and we'd learn the bass parts as well as guitar parts for every record we could lay our hands on. We had similar abilities and we were happy playing and singing in harmony together.

Eric formed the group The Elements and I was asked to join them, playing guitar and bass, swapping with Eric, so that really was the start of my bass playing.

My parents came along to hear us play in rehearsal at Eric's parent's house. Dad asked what we were going to play and Eric replied, mumbling something that sounded like, 'Tillawizoo'. Dad said that he'd never heard 'Tillawizoo' and he didn't know the song until we started to play and Eric sang the opening lines:

There were bells, on a hill,
But I never heard them ringing,
No I never heard them at all
Tillawizoo

Of course, Eric had said, 'Till There Was You', Dad had just misheard it.

It's strange how some silly memories come back from nowhere. In 1986 while on tour with Elton, I asked drummer Charlie Morgan if I could look at his set list just so that I could reference it with mine. A song on his list that I didn't recognise was 'Ndongo', I asked him what it was and he sang: 'Ndongo Breaking My Heart'.

I digress.

Tilly and Pop

My Granny from my mother's side was Tilly Thomson and I'm named after my Grandad, David Thomson. They were a couple of real Edinburgh characters; they were very down-to-earth, with no airs or graces. Tilly was an excellent seamstress and Pop Thomson had been a railwayman all his working days. He was a very happy man and seemed to be very content with his life, enjoying his retirement. The only thing that got him riled was politics (the taxman, Mr Heath). Tilly was the matriarch and it was at her house in Springwell Place that the family would gather. There were never any planned events, it was just the place to go and there were always friends or family visiting. It was certainly a lunchtime haunt for all of us. There was always something cooking: hot soup, tea, toast, square sliced sausage cooked in an inch of lard. Practically anything could be mustered up fairly quickly. But it was delicious and I spent many happy hours in Springwell Place with family or playing dominoes with whoever fancied a game, 'chappin''(the word used when unable to make a play) being the cry.

I had been shopping with Tilly one snowy January day and as we walked back to Springwell Place, she asked me to go ahead of her and open the door. As I walked ahead through the snow, I heard a thump behind me and Tilly saying, 'That's me doon'. I turned around to see her sitting in the snow with a big smile on her face 'aye that's me doon' she said as she was lifted to her feet by some helpful pedestrians.

Pop used very similar language. My dad was driving to the off licence to get the drinks order in for New Year. He took Pop with him and Dougal (our pet Cairn terrier) sat on Pop's knee. Pop rolled the window down because Dougal was panting a bit and he thought that the fresh air would help Dougal settle. Dad negotiated a roundabout and as he drove on, he heard Pop say 'that's the dug away, Jack'. Dougal had seen a dog on the grass verge and like any other dog, was not really in control of his emotions, so he jumped out the window. No harm was done, and the dog was fine.

'Aye that's the dug away, Jack'.

My parents had a habit of telling me that their best friends were actually aunts and uncles, 'This is your Uncle Jimmy and Auntie June' it was nonsense and very confusing for me, as I wasn't really sure who my real aunts and uncles were.

I certainly never really understood how I had a black Aunt Sophie from South Africa. Sophie was Tilly's best pal, and I often saw her at Springwell Place. A lovely, big woman, warm and friendly, she was always laughing and a good storyteller. She was a fascinating character, and it's still not clear to me where or how they first met, but it was a lifelong friendship. When I took my girlfriend Mary to meet Tilly and Pop, it was at a New Year family get-together. Tilly was teetotal and the family wouldn't dare ask for a beer, wine or spirit. Several family members were there that evening and we were asked in turn what we wanted to drink. 'Oh, a wee cup o' tea will be fine for me Tilly', or 'I'll have a glass of lemonade', or 'Coca Cola for me, please'. I hadn't mentioned to Mary that Tilly was teetotal, so when she asked Mary what she would like to drink, Mary, totally unaware, said 'Vodka and Coke, please'. 'Aye nae bother hen', was the reply. There were stunned looks on all the faces and a wee snigger from me.

Every time Pop said, 'I'm away doon fir a paper' he'd be having a quick nip and a pint with a pocket full of peppermints to disguise the tell-tale waft on his breath, but he'd always arrive back with an *Evening News* tucked under his arm and the only give away was the flushed face and that wry smile.

As I mentioned earlier, Tilly's best friend was Aunt Sophie, who was South African. Tilly always said what she thought and because she was a little bit deaf, it was usually in a loud voice. When Pop was ill and had to be hospitalised, he was tended to by an African nurse with markings on her face. As the nurse walked towards us, Tilly said to me, 'She's a real darky that one, Davie'. She didn't mean any harm; it was just the way she spoke. This was the way most of that generation spoke and I don't believe there was any malice in it. Saying things like 'I'm away to the Paki's for a packet of fags', or 'let's have a Chinky tonight' – they were all acceptable expressions back in the 60s. Thankfully, we're all a bit more PC now and most of us are aware of how insulting these old terms sound in this day and age. However, while living in London, I was called Jock or Scotty on many occasions, and it didn't bother me.

Pop had a fall at home and an ambulance was called and took him to hospital. They kept him in for observation. I drove Tilly to see him as often as possible; he became very confused and he was convinced that his brother Alan was sitting at the bottom of the bed. On more than one occasion, he was heard to say, 'Alan, what are you doing here'. There was also an imaginary pipe that he kept asking me to pass to him. His ward was next to the maternity one and he said to us one day, 'that's three gone up and two come doon'. We later found out that three people had died on his ward and two births had taken place at the maternity ward next door. How he knew that I'll never know. Sadly, Pop succumbed to septicaemia after a month and Tilly followed him within the year.

Mrs Whitehead (a visiting clairvoyant) attended the house for a séance with my mum and a few of her friends from work. I briefly stepped into the living room, where they were all sitting, drinking tea and chatting. Mum introduced me to Mrs Whitehead. She had such a friendly face and smiled at me and shook my hand. Later, my mum told me that Mrs Whitehead asked her if I played the banjo; mum told her I played the guitar, and Mrs Whitehead said I'd do well with my guitar playing. I find it fascinating that some people are gifted with that sixth sense.

The Paton family

This is a poem my dad Jack wrote after a battle he was involved in. It took place in Fontenay la Pesnel, Normandy, June 1944.

O Laddie if I had my way
You'd probably be here today

But that day in a far-off land
You came at me wi' gun in hand
And though your courage wasn't failing
I am a Scot and not for nailing
Hardly was your first shot fired
Than your own short life expired
For as my own Bard said sae dour
'Thou met me in an evil hour'

We both were only twenty then
Not young boys but not quite men
Proud to serve our country too
Each believing our cause was true
I wonder what your mother thought
When the news to her was brought
Her tall young babe wi' golden hair
Lay asleep somewhere out there
I wonder if we'd never met
If you would still be living yet
Or if your shot had been more true
It might be me out there not you.

There was talent in the Paton family. As well as writing the occasional poem, my Dad (Jack) did a lot of singing around the clubs and he was a great lover of opera. He was also a Robert Burns fanatic and adored Sinatra, of course. Mum danced and won a few competitions at the Palais in Fountain Bridge. It was well known that she'd danced with Sir Sean Connery and according to mum, he even chatted her up. By contrast, my sister Nina can't sing for toffee, but it doesn't stop her trying. I value that, as she likes fun and I enjoy her company.

Dad would sing at the drop of a hat, no accompaniment necessary. Mary and I would often pop down to visit my parents on Sunday afternoon. We'd finished our afternoon tea and while mum was washing up, dad was putting some glasses away in the drinks cabinet. There was a slight lull in the conversation and without warning, he turned around and burst into the opening lines of 'Sorrento', 'Video mare quant'e bello'. He just wanted to sing and it must have seemed like an appropriate time to entertain us. There was no shyness or lack of confidence with my Dad; he knew he was a gifted singer and so did we.

He also had a gift for clairvoyance. He was very reluctant to use his gift and said it was wrong to try to communicate with the spirit world. But he could do it and it wasn't always a pleasant experience. All kinds of spirits can visit an Ouija board and the Paton's witnessed some scary events but also some amazing things. He told me he had a Native American spirit guide – he'd seen him. Dad passed away in November 1989 while on holiday in Florida, very close to the Big Cypress Seminole Indian Reservation. That same year in December, I was looking for music to play at Hogmanay. I found a cassette tape I didn't recognise and put it into the player. I was amazed to hear my Dad sing 'Auld Lang Syne' at the press of the play button. I hadn't wound it back or forward – I just pressed play and the song started. It was a bit spooky, but I listened to him singing to the end of the song. I felt that he was with me again for a few precious moments.

We had many musical evenings where the singers would sing unaccompanied. My Uncle Dodie (not a real uncle but still family) was also a good singer and it was always a special treat to hear him sing Jack Jones or Frank Sinatra. My guitar playing was coming on really well and when Dodie launched into 'Fly Me To The Moon', I picked up my guitar and accompanied him – yes, I was gaining confidence. When he finished, he said to me that that was the best accompaniment he had ever had for that song. These words of encouragement came at the right time for me particularly as it was from someone I had a lot of respect for. From then on, the guitar was always with me for family sing-songs. I still didn't have the confidence to sing for them, but I could play my guitar and feel more involved with the entertainment and a bit happier that they didn't need to sing without accompaniment.

Grandpa (George) Paton and Granny (Helen), my Dad's parents, were very clairvoyant. He was a non-commissioned officer in the First World War. They were a big family and sadly, two of my uncles lost their lives in the Second World War. Dad was badly injured while serving in France and had some shrapnel wounds in his elbow that prevented him from being able to play a musical instrument. He told me that a shell landed in a trench he was in with a few of his army buddies; he was the only survivor. He also said that he felt the Germans had concentrated all their firepower on him and he tried to bury himself in the earth to escape the bombardment. How lucky our generation is not to have to experience such horrors.

Occasionally on a Sunday, George and Helen would have a séance at home. Apparently, these were very advanced séances which included materialisation and voices. I was too young to witness any of this, but Mum and Dad told me a bit about it when I was older.

On one visit to my grandparents' house when I was three or four years old, I was asked to sing for them. I was even shy back then and held on to mum's skirt, sucking my thumb and shaking my head. Somehow, they persuaded me to sing a Roy Rogers song, 'A Four-legged Friend'. I said I'd do it if I could stand in the cupboard and sing – some cowboy! The adults thought this was a great idea, so into the cupboard, I went. 'OK, David, off you go, son, whenever you're ready'. And so I began:

A four-legged friend
A four-legged friend
He'll never let you down,
He's honest and faithful right up to the end
My wonderful one two three four-legged friend.

Written by: Bob Hope & Jimmy Wakely – 1952

First Bands

1966 to 1968. The Beachcombers

I left school at 15 and Mum had me lined up for a job as an apprentice mechanic. I lasted three days, not helped by my mates sitting on the wall outside shouting and laughing every time I appeared with a broom in my hands sweeping the floor. I thought I'd be at least changing spark plugs and was a bit disillusioned, to say the least. On the 3rd day, I'd had enough and come lunchtime, I joined the guys on the wall and we set off to Liberton dams, where we pitched a tent, lit a fire, smoked cigarettes and had a brew of hot Bovril. Alcohol or getting high wasn't something that interested us at that age.

I needed to earn my keep and had a few jobs. I worked at an electrical wholesalers and the fruit market and I also did a couple of months at an upholsterer. Although I lasted more than three days, none of the jobs held any interest for me and I hated getting up early in the morning to go to work. I just wanted to make music. My sister saw an ad in the *Evening News* for a lead guitarist. We set off together to the phone box to call the number – we didn't have the luxury of a house phone in 1965. The band was The Beachcombers and the auditions were being held at the Gonk Club in Tollcross. I didn't have an amp or a decent guitar, but my sister's fiancé was Ally Black, lead guitarist with The Athenians. He drove me to the club with his Selmer amp and Fender Stratocaster in the boot of the car, all ready for me to do the audition. It was my first and I had to stand on stage with the band and play through a few songs. I didn't know if I was good enough to play in a band back then, but I knew I needed to do this audition. I played the songs just as I'd learned them. They liked me and they liked my playing. The band had a chat and asked me to wait by the stage. After a few minutes, they approached me and said that I'd passed the audition and they wanted me as their lead guitarist; I couldn't believe my luck.

The Beachcombers were one of Edinburgh's top bands and the choice of music they played was excellent. Their repertoire was based around soul and r & b. Songs in the set included 'In the Midnight Hour', 'Mr Pitiful', 'Ain't Too Proud to Beg', 'The Tracks of My Tears', '6345789 That's My Number', 'I'm a Soul Man' and 'Baby I Need Your Lovin'. At last, I was in a band; this is where I wanted to be and I was loving it. They were an established group and there was no shortage of gigs. We travelled the length and breadth of Scotland playing town halls, church halls, ballrooms and clubs. Gigs seemed to be everywhere. There are websites that cover this era in Scotland and for me, they make fascinating reading. (See www.edinphoto.org.uk)

Mr Kenny McLean senior managed The Beachcombers and his son Kenny junior was the drummer. Kenny senior and I didn't really see eye to eye. He didn't rate me and told me I would never be a successful musician as I didn't have the right attitude. But the guys were great, Kenny junior was the one who always spoke up for me and I seemed to fit the bill as far as the band was concerned. At that time, I was young and enthusiastic, and I realised I could play to a fairly good standard for my age. I was only 16, and I felt that having the right attitude was something that would develop over time and with the experience that I was definitely lacking.

But having fun has always been important to me, and outside of my work with the band, I was running wild, meeting lots of people, new friends and new acquaintances, some good and some not so good.

On one occasion, I remember having a crazy night with the Stock Pot crowd (the name of a café on Lothian Road). Someone had purple hearts. These were Amphetamines and I had my first and last experience with them as they were passed about like sweets. We were all full of energy and buzzing. I didn't want to go home to my parents' house, so a friend took me to a house in Niddry. The tenant of the house was a girl named Sheila. After seeing the condition I was in, she recommended I spend the night and try to sleep off my drug-induced state. Her spare room was occupied by a pretty girl – a dancer, I think. She was already in bed when Sheila knocked on her door and asked her if I could share her bed; she asked for the light to be turned on, looked at me and said ok. Unfortunately, the purple hearts had taken their toll and any chance of having fun was going to be a bit of a challenge. Despite her persistent and interesting attempts at stimulation, it was a complete and utter failure. But it was fun and we had a laugh trying to wake up Mr Floppy. Come the morning, and everything was back in working order. After breakfast, I walked her to the bus stop, said goodbye and never saw her again. I walked part of the way home and then jumped on a bus the rest of the way. I collapsed into bed as soon as I reached my bedroom.

The band had a rehearsal later that day, and I was late as I'd overslept. I felt terrible, so maybe Kenny McLean's views on my attitude at that time were justified. But hey! I was 16, living and learning all the way and there's nothing better than a hands-on experience.

Our singer Mike Rowberry was studying at Napier College and he invited a girl he knew along to hear the band. She was Rose Burnett. She liked the band and I saw her at a couple of gigs. After a while, she started to come to the gigs with her twin sister. They were identical and very attractive. Rose introduced her twin as Mary. They were very eye-catching – blonde, blue-eyed, five foot two, with high cheekbones. They were absolutely gorgeous.

Ian Doyle and John Smith became our roadies for a while and we often remarked on the twins. As well as working with the band, Ian and I did a lot of socialising together. While at a Chris Farlow gig at McGoos in the High Street, we met the twins who were coming downstairs from the café. We chatted for a while as people bustled past us. Mary was accidentally bumped into and stumbled on the stair, I caught her in my arms and that seemed to be a significant moment. As it was safer on the dance floor than standing on the stair, off we went. Ian was a fantastic dancer and I think Rose was thrilled. But me? I just bounced from one foot to the other very self-consciously, wondering who was watching me. We walked the girls home after the show and then Ian and I walked back home to The Inch, it was a good six-mile walk and took us a couple of hours, but that seemed to be the norm in those days. We did a lot of walking back then. Mary became my regular girlfriend and we'd meet at least two or three nights a week.

Gigs were great with The Beachcombers, the girls liked us and the guys liked us too. Many fans of the band would travel by bus to see us at gigs outside Edinburgh. We did well and after a couple of years, we wanted to push our horizons a bit further.

Somehow, we got to hear of an audition in The Marquee Club, Wardour Street, London. It was for CBS records and they were looking for new talent. It sounds mad to me now, but we drove all the way to London in a cramped Austin J4. I don't know how we did it, so Kenny senior must have driven some of us in his car, as I can't imagine five band members, a driver and a manager, plus all our gear in the one Austin J4! Somehow, we managed, although we did arrive a little late. They agreed to let us play because of the distance we had travelled. We passed the audition and as well as a recording contract, we were offered a residency at the Marquee every second Sunday. This seemed like a great opportunity for us, so we returned to Edinburgh and made arrangements to make the move to London. A flat was found in Redcliff Gardens, Kensington and we secured the rental for a year.

London was a real eye-opener. Five young guys from Edinburgh living in a huge ground-floor flat – we sure had fun. The Earls Court area was a great place to be and there were many strange new sites for us. None of us were drinkers, but we'd occasionally visit the pub at the bottom of the street. It was called The Cauldron, and it was fine downstairs – just a regular pub. We ventured upstairs and quickly realised it was a gay bar! The London gays were pretty outrageous, flamboyant and confident and it was obviously more acceptable to display your sexual preference in London than in Edinburgh at that time. There were cross-dressers and guys getting off buses in leathers carrying motorbike helmets – what was that all about? But there was something in the air, a feeling that something was happening. All around us, there was an awakening in music, culture, in attitude, and we couldn't be in a better place to watch it unfold. We became friends with a Glasgow band named The House of Lords. Vocalist Rab Munro would often visit us and he introduced us to the delights of smoking pot.

Robin Le Mesurier heard us play at a club in Kensington; he really liked the band and invited us along to meet his Mum and Stepfather. His mum was Hattie Jacques and his father was John Le Mesurier. Robin dropped by the flat a few times. He arrived one evening and told us that his mother wanted to meet us and had kindly invited us to dinner the following evening. That came as a nice surprise, and we were all eager to meet Hattie. It was a huge surprise and thrill to arrive at the house and be greeted by Hattie's husband, John Schofield. Although Hattie had previously been married to John Le Mesurier, they had divorced in 1963. It was a fantastic, entertaining evening, and Hattie and John were very kind to us. We left the house laden with games, gifts, and a wonderful memory of an evening with Hattie. I'm very grateful to Robin for setting it up. I was to meet him again when I was with Pilot.

CBS had a tie-up with Shapiro Bernstein music publishers and we were sent along there to listen to songs that might be suitable for us to record. They played us a song called 'Even The Bad Times Are Good' written by Mitch Murray and Pete Callander. We loved the song – it had hit written all over it. A studio date was arranged, and we recorded the song with Pete and Mitch producing. Unfortunately, their recording proficiency was not really up to professional standards, although we were delighted to be in a London studio, playing and recording our first single. We were all geared up for the song to be pressed and released when we received the disappointing news that The Tremeloes wanted to record the song, so we were denied permission to release it. Instead, we had to return to Shapiro Bernstein and find another song. That was a stroke of bad luck as we had *The Tony Blackburn TV Show* lined up to help promote the release. It was a double blow to watch the Tremeloes climb the charts with our song. It reached number four in UK and 36 in the USA.

We really wanted another song from Pete and Mitch, but they were on a roll and we didn't really figure in their plans. So, another song was found called 'The Animal in Me', which was originally an Italian song that was translated into English for us. Time seemed to drag on until another date was set for recording, but when we arrived at the studio, we were surprised to see session players ready to play the song for us. There was also another band there called The Mud; they were there to record a song called 'Up the Airy Mountain' which was released on CBS records in March 1968. Oh, dear! I still remember hearing them sing 'Up the airy mountain down the rushing glen'. Our bass player Sandy was talking to one of their guys and he said, 'so you've got session players, too?' Sandy replied, 'aye, but we're going to replace their parts when they finish'. 'Ha ha, aye, right'. We had no chance.

The name of our band was also changed to Boots because The Beachcombers name was already registered. 'The Animal in Me' was eventually released in 1968, and not surprisingly, it didn't get much airplay. Our next release was 'Keep Your Love Light Burning', another flop.

Our booking agent Ron was one of those flamboyant gays who we found quite amusing at the time. You must remember that being gay was rarely discussed back then and something of a curiosity to us – it was a criminal offence in the UK until 1967. We invited Ron round to the flat one night for a drink and a chat – I think he had a crush on Mike, our vocalist. Ron liked his wine, so we bought some for him, but we made the mistake of asking him personal questions about his sex life and we probably went a bit overboard. He left our flat a little drunk, a little angry and a bit insulted. The next day we got a message from his office saying he wouldn't be working with us anymore.

That left us with no gigs. Sandy wanted to return to Scotland and who could blame him? He was replaced by Dougie McKendrick on bass; it was all beginning to fall apart. CBS told us they didn't have any more songs for us and if we wanted to have a chance at success, we should start to write songs of our own. I remember sitting with Dougie, trying to write songs, but we didn't really have a clue how to do it.

Everything seemed to be going badly for Boots. We even had the van broken into and all our gear stolen. Mr McLean suggested pawning our rings or anything of value, I had a gold ring that Tilly had bought me, but there was no way I would pawn it. The future looked a bit shaky for Boots. The flat in Redcliff Gardens had to go and the guys moved into digs while I moved in with my sister, who had a flat in Anselm Road, Chelsea.

Nina is a joy to be with and, at the time, had a great number of hippy pals who would drop by for an evening. She was a real 60s chick. She worked in a boutique called BIBA and was chosen to do a bit of modelling for the clothes that BIBA sold. One of her pals was a wee bit wacky and came around to read some poetry for us. He introduced himself to me as Chris Jagger; my sis said it was true – he was Mick Jagger's brother. He sat down on the couch and produced a children's book by Dr Seuss from his canvas shoulder bag. He opened the book and began by looking at me and asking the question, 'What do you know about Tweedle Beetles?' I said I didn't know anything. 'Well' he said, 'when Tweedle Beetles fight, it's called a Tweedle Beetle battle (pause) and when Tweedle Beetles fight in a puddle, it's called a Tweedle Beetle puddle battle'. He looked up to make sure he had my attention. He continued, 'and when Tweedle Beetles fight in a puddle with paddles, it's called a Tweedle Beetle puddle paddle battle'. This made me laugh out loud. But he wasn't laughing; this was serious stuff, so he just scowled at me. He then returned to his book and continued to read, ignoring me while I had tears of laughter streaming down my face. It wasn't funny to him; it was intended as an education on the habits of The Tweedle Beetle.

The Beatles were here, there and everywhere. *The White Album* came out at that time and I spent many hours listening and learning how to play the songs, although, in the years to come, Paul McCartney would go on to show me I had the wrong guitar inversions for *Blackbird*.

Gigs had dried up completely for Boots, so we had to get out and find day jobs. I began to see the guys less and less and would only call once or twice a week.

I signed on with Manpower employment agency; they were great and had a fine selection of jobs available. My first job was with The South African Wine Farmers Association in Tower Bridge. I liked it there, although all I remember doing was sticking labels on the wine bottles. I enjoyed the attention from the girls who liked my Scottish accent, they called me Jock and I enjoyed the way they would say it in their cockney accents, 'hello

Jock, where's your kilt'. But it was a full-time job and a long tube journey from Earls Court to Tower Bridge, so I probably lasted a month.

Next, I was given a job with the BBC delivering equipment to various studios throughout London. This was a really interesting and cushy job; it was part-time, and I would meet the BBC delivery van at Hammersmith. I had a BBC pass and could wander round the studios watching what was going on. I stumbled across the recording for the *Lulu Show* one day and watched her going through the rehearsals. Lulu was given her own BBC One TV series in 1968, which ran until 1975 under various titles, including *Lulu's Back in Town*, *Happening for Lulu*, *It's Lulu* and *Lulu*.

I stood by the studio door and watched for ten minutes or so. The director announced a break and Lulu came walking toward the studio door I was standing at. As she walked past me, she gave me a long look and a big smile and said hello, which made my day! I was to meet her again at Elton's 50th birthday party, where she was introduced to me by Davey Johnstone.

But the band wanted to move back to Edinburgh and make a new start. Mike (our singer) had already gone back because of pressure from his girlfriend, Elise. Disillusioned, disappointed and at a dead end, we sorted our affairs and one by one, we returned to Edinburgh. I was the last to leave London and was in two minds about returning, but I missed playing, so I made the journey back home to Scotland. We did get back together for a few gigs without Mike and Sandy, who had both moved on and the gigs were well received, but the energy and enthusiasm had gone out of the band. It wasn't the same without Mike as our front man and Sandy on bass, so we eventually went our separate ways. It's a pity that we didn't find the luck that we really needed; we certainly gave it our best shot. But as one chapter comes to an end, another begins.

1969. The Bay City Rollers

I first saw Tam Paton (no relation) at the Palais Ballroom in Fountainbridge, Edinburgh, one Saturday afternoon when I was about 15 years old. He had his own band initially, called The Crusaders, and then he formed The Tam Paton Orchestra. He looked like a pop star as I watched him make his way to the stage, escorted by one of the staff. He would sit at the piano but mainly concentrated on conducting the band. I was fascinated and spent a lot of the time watching what was happening on stage.

We met again when he brought The Bay City Rollers, who he managed, along to hear The Beachcombers play at the International Club in Princes

Street. He wanted the Rollers to see us and maybe learn something from watching us; in a way he was modelling the Rollers on The Beachcombers, I suppose, which was quite a compliment. We dressed well, usually in white suits, we were very professional and we had good communication with our audience. I was surprised to see The Rollers and I could tell that they were watching and enjoying what they saw and heard.

Incidentally, the Roller's name came about after one of the guys closed their eyes and pointed at a map of the USA and it turned out that his finger landed on a place called Bay City. They found out that the waves that crashed on the beach at Bay City were called Bay City Rollers, but you possibly already guessed that!

With the demise of The Beachcombers / Boots, I needed work and quickly. Thomas Paton and Sons was a well-established potato merchant based in Prestonpans, East Lothian. Tam Paton was one of the sons and was named after his father, the elder son coincidentally being called David Paton. Tam wanted to talk with me, so we met at Tollcross while he was delivering to the local greengrocer. I sat in the lorry with him – just Tam, me and his dog, Tweed. He asked me what I was up to and I told him I was out of a job; I needed some kind of work to tide me over. He said I could help him with the deliveries, which seemed like a good idea to me. I accepted the job and having the same surname, I felt like I was part of the family. 'Go on, tell them your name', Tam would say as we talked to the Italian chip shop owners. I enjoyed the work as it was physical and I felt like it was getting me fit. Tam spoke about The Rollers all the time. He kept saying that I should come along and hear them play, but I kept declining.

We'd just finished delivering to a grocer shop when we were hassled by a traffic warden and the lorry had to be moved. Tam had some business to do with the store, so he said to me, 'drive the lorry roond the block'. 'What?' 'Aye, take it roond the block, you'll be fine'. I didn't have a heavy goods vehicle licence; I was 17 and it was a big lorry laden with bags of tatties and I'd never driven anything bigger than a Morris Minor! It was a nightmare and when I stopped at the traffic lights on an uphill slope, I couldn't find first gear. The light changed to green and the lorry kept rolling back as I struggled with the gear changer, with the drivers behind becoming very angry, beeping their horns and shouting and swearing at me to 'get a fucking move on'. Tweed' was giving me funny looks and getting very agitated. I thought he was going to do a Dougal on me and jump out the window, but I found first gear eventually and made it safely back to the grocer shop. It was pretty stressful, though.

After a couple of months of carrying 25kg bags of potatoes, I started to develop muscles I never knew I had. Life was good and I was happy with the work, apart from wanting to get back in a band. I was content, though and enjoyed my days working with Tam and delivering to grocers and fish and chip shops in and around Edinburgh.

While delivering to The Deep Sea, which was a well-known chippy on Leith Walk, I was really surprised to see Chris Jagger from London – the Tweedle Beetle guy. He was standing on the pavement just a few feet away and had obviously been watching me. He wore a green velvet jacket, a hat with a feather in it, beads around his neck, loon pants (flared denim trousers) and sandals. He was staring at me with a big grin on his face. I said hello to him and asked him what he was doing in Edinburgh. He said, 'I've come to see you, David'. I smiled nervously, trying to make sense of what he said. I found it a bit creepy the way he stared at me with a half-smile; there was that stoned look on his face that made me feel uneasy. Luckily, Tam appeared and that was my cue to make my escape. I said we had to rush to the next delivery. I couldn't wait to get in the lorry and on to the next stop.

Sergio had a fish and chip shop in Tollcross. I still hear him saying, 'Tatty Tam, fackeen City Bay Rollers eez all you talk, why you no talk tatties!'. He was a character. He was always unhappy about the price and would become very irate and shout, swear and get very red in the face as he argued with Tam. But Tam was always polite and kept his cool; after all, the customer is always right. Sergio did sometimes give me a bag of chips and a smile, so he wasn't all bad.

I liked Tam, and I had a lot of respect for his drive and dedication to The Rollers. He was a very charismatic guy and when he was out and about with the bands, he was always sharply dressed. He usually wore a grey hand-tailored suit and Beatle Boots specially ordered from Anello & Davide in London. He drove a white Zephyr 6 and was every inch a band manager. While sitting in the lorry having lunch, he asked me again if I'd be interested in joining the band, and I said no, I don't really want to be a Roller. I wanted to push myself musically and I didn't think I'd be stretched with them, but Tam was very persuasive, very persistent and a great salesman too. The Rollers did have a kind of mystique about them that aroused my curiosity. I had lots of questions and Tam had all the answers; he offered to buy me a new Gibson Les Paul, a Marshall amp, to give me a clothes allowance, a good wage and gigs five nights a week. It was beginning to sound irresistible. How could I turn down an offer like that? He definitely saw me as an asset to The Rollers. OK, it was worth a shot, even for a year or so, and I had nothing else on the go. So Tam took me along to a Rollers gig. I was impressed, they sounded good and they were very popular. The guys were great; they had Nobby Clark on vocals, Alan Longmuir on bass, his younger brother Derek on drums and Keith Norman on keys. Greg was on guitar and he was the guy I'd be replacing. They interpreted the chart songs of that era very well.

I couldn't have asked for a nicer bunch of guys to work with. Their enthusiasm was intense and their thoughts were always on the band and how to make it even more successful. However, at the time the guys all had day jobs. Alan was a Plumber, Nobby and Derek were carpenters and Keith was in college. I also heard that Keith joined the navy after he left The Rollers. Tam was very strict with us and girlfriends were definitely taboo. Any free time was allocated to rehearsal, a night at the cinema or a Chinese meal. Tam really wanted to keep us occupied and make sure no relationships had a chance of developing. Mary and I had split up at the time and I wasn't seeing any other girl, so I followed the rules for a while.

I took a bit of stick from some other musician friends for joining The Rollers, but I couldn't really criticise the band in any way. I heard all the negative comments and put them down to jealousy as The Rollers were hugely popular. They were good at what they did and I just wanted to help make them even better if I could. They had my full attention and I was as focused as any of them. I was caught up in Roller mania, but I wanted to make a good job of it. There is no point in doing something half-heartedly.

The music was left in our hands while Tam was out there working hard to make the hopes and dreams come true. Girls were everywhere, and with that came a lot of envy from guys, so it became a bit of a problem. Having so many screaming girls was bound to create aggression from the boys and we got plenty. On more than one occasion, we had to make a mad dash for the car being chased by screaming girls who wanted to rip our clothes off and jealous guys who wanted to kick the shit out of us. One time a numpty even managed to get his arm in the open window of the car trying to take a swipe at Alan, who grabbed on to him and held him while thumping him in the face as we sped down the road. It wasn't until he started screaming that he let him go! There was no messin' with Alan; he could handle himself in his own quiet way. I always found Alan to be very modest, kind, and a good, fun guy. He was a smart dresser, too – all his suits were made to measure.

On the other hand, Tam was a tough guy and very fit. If a fight broke out at a gig, Tam would step into the crowd and try to put an end to it. I saw a guy flying over a piano at the side of the stage after a thump from him. That side of the business was a bit tiresome and relentless, but it's the price you pay for being in a band that has a huge female following. I even remember walking down the street and two guys behind me saying, 'that's the guy from The Rollers – let's batter him'. You have to laugh.

Derek was very shy and difficult to converse with, but he was always smiling and had a happy-go-lucky way about him. Neither Alan nor Derek were going to be breaking any boundaries with their musical ability, but they loved what they were doing and put in so many hours working on their playing and you had to admire them for that. I've worked with a few great players in my time, but I still consider dedication as being one of the key ingredients to success. That's where The Rollers beat every other band, hands down because nobody could compete with that amount of enthusiasm.

Nobby was the perfect frontman for the band as it was then. He was always well-rehearsed and had very good musical ability. We became really good pals and remain so to this day. All in all, it was a happy band and it's mainly happy memories about them that spring to mind.

I was the only member of the band to hold a driving licence and was in charge of the van for a while. I parked it outside 16 Valleyfield Street, Tollcross, where I lived with my parents. But girls were always hanging about the stair. We were just an Edinburgh band in those days, but we created hysteria at every gig. On one occasion, I was at home. I'd just had a shower and was crossing from the shower room to my bedroom, so I was naked. I looked toward the door and heard the letterbox close and girls giggling outside; they must have seen me in the altogether while peeking through the letterbox. Well, I never!

We played a gig at the Cavendish and I saw Mary there with a friend. She looked gorgeous, but I didn't get a chance to say hello. That would have been impossible and the fans would have ripped her apart, but I did write to her and included my phone number, asking her to call me. She did call, but I didn't receive it as my Mum thought she was a fan and put the phone down on her. But she did write and explained what had happened. I told Mum that if Mary phoned again, I wanted to speak with her. At last, we spoke and although it was difficult to date, I arranged to pick her up after a gig. Tam always followed me home and made sure the van was locked up securely before saying goodnight, so I waited till he left, then jumped in the van and made my way to Mary's house. It became a pattern, but Tam got wise to it and followed me one night. I picked Mary up and as we drove along Granton Road, I noticed he was behind me. I stopped and watched him through the rear-view mirror as he emerged from his car. He came to the window and said, 'hello Mary, how are you?', and with a wry smile on his face, he looked at me as if to say, I got you. 'I'll see YOU tomorrow'.

We had a gig at Frisco's in The High Street that Sunday afternoon. Well, that was a laugh. The dressing room was at the opposite end of the hall from the stage and we had to run the gauntlet to get to the stage. On the way back to the dressing rooms, we were all set upon by throngs of screaming girls trying to kiss us and pull at our clothes. Hands were everywhere and one of them had her hand on my crotch. She was holding on tight and I couldn't move – I was pinned to the spot by a gaggle of girls. They were all pulling and kissing me, so I couldn't tell which one had her hand on my privates. I was shouting, 'who's doing that? Stop it, right now; I'm calling the police'. I couldn't move my arms to ward them off; all they wanted to do was get a piece of us and pull our hair and plant sloppy kisses on our poor, ravaged bodies. Things were getting out of hand. It sounds funny and exciting, and I suppose it really was, but there were times when it became a pain and a little embarrassing. Eventually, we were rescued by Tam and the roadies. In the dressing room (when we got our breath back), I was ticked off in front of The Rollers and in front of another band Tandem, whom Tam also managed, for disobeying the rules about girlfriends. Still, I wasn't the only guilty one, Archie Marr from Tandem had also been caught by Tam with a girl, but it really was looked upon as breaking the rules.

But we had fun with The Rollers, great fun. Horse riding became a monthly event and we'd ride across the Pentland Hills from the stables in Penicuik. Swimming was popular too; we swam in the Firth of Forth, near Cockenzie and I can assure you, it's fuckin' freezin'. It's beginning to sound like a regular boy's club and I suppose it was, in a way. We decided we'd take a couple of weeks out and drive to Spain. A roof rack was bought for the Transit van, loads of provisions were purchased from the cash and carry and we headed south. We had nothing booked; we just set off, followed the map and hoped for the best. The first year we made it as far as Le Mans, France. That was as far as we got. The van was overheating and the mechanic who looked at it said it was a weight problem combined with the outside temperature. We had to slowly make our way back to the UK. On our return, we dropped by my sister's flat in London. She was living hand to mouth at that time, so we left her with lots of leftovers that we didn't need. She and her pal Jacqui thought it was Christmas and were laughing with joy.

The next year we tried again with a bigger van; we made it all the way to Lloret de Mar in Spain. It was excellent fun, horse riding on the beach, swimming, sleeping under the stars and cooking on the primus stove.

Keith Norman quit the band, so we needed another band member. It was decided that we'd go for a rhythm guitarist instead of a keyboard player. Tam had a habit of recommending other guys to augment the band. Eric was one name that springs to mind, a really nice guy who couldn't play the guitar at all. I tried to give him a couple of lessons, but he was thrown in at the deep end. I just tied his guitar lead around the handle of my amp because there was no input for him to plug into. It was embarrassing when it was noticed by the guys who wandered down the front, pointing to the lead and laughing. I felt for Eric as he was invited to join the band by Tam and not many guys would say no to the chance of getting up on stage and having a crack at it with such a popular band. It didn't bother the girls because he was a great-looking guy, but it bothered me. This was my big objection to the direction of the band, I wanted to raise the level of our musical ability, but it didn't seem to be important to Tam. 'Just look the part and smile a lot', he'd say. I wasn't happy. I liked Eric but making good music was important to me. Looking good might be a bonus, but playing well should be the priority with any band that wants to be taken seriously. Imagine working on a building site and the plumber looks great, but he doesn't know the first thing about pipes!

Eric didn't stay for long. Tam said he had found a guy, a keyboard player. He brought him along to a rehearsal. This is how I first met Billy Lyall. He had been a flautist with the Royal Marines Band and was a classically trained musician, but he never had a clue how to play pop/rock music, 'what's a 12 bar' he'd say. I was ready to give up on him until I walked into Alan and Derek's house one day, as we'd always meet there before setting off to a gig. Billy was at the piano playing a piece of Bach and I was stunned to hear such accomplished playing from him – he was brilliant. I sat beside him and asked him to play some more, it was effortless to him and he rattled off some pretty difficult pieces. I distinctly remember him playing 'The Arrival of the Queen of Sheba', a very accomplished piece of music written by Handel. I knew then that Billy did have excellent musical ability and I could help him with his improvisation on a 12-bar. He was a quick learner and started to shine within a short period of time.

It was Billy who helped me improve my sight reading and encouraged me to join the library on George the IV Bridge, Edinburgh. We would walk there once a month and obtain duets for guitar and flute from the music department. I soon reached the stage of being able to play intermediate pieces for classical guitar. His flute playing was of a very high standard and he had a great deal of patience with me, so I was soon able to tackle the works of my favourite baroque composer J S Bach and I adored playing him. I had hours of fun playing things I'd never heard before. Billy had opened my eyes to music I thought I'd never be able to tackle. What a thrill it is to read music, not knowing what's coming next until you play it, and the feeling of accomplishment was immense. I've always been good at focusing and achieving the goals that I strive for, especially with anything musical and I felt really proud that I could do something that was out of the norm for your average rock musician. It served me well with session work in years to come. I watched Billy flourish, his playing and improvisation improved very quickly and we were miles ahead of everyone in our thirst for all things musical.

I wanted to progress and I felt that I couldn't move forward any further on the path The Rollers wanted to pursue. I was looking for a change. Tam went off to London for a week and tried to muster some interest in the band. He succeeded and it was arranged that some A&R guys would be coming up to hear and see us. It was crazy now and we couldn't go anywhere or do anything without being mobbed by screaming girls. The A&R guys appeared at a gig and one of them looked very dodgy. He had a trench coat, blonde hair, small round glasses and eyes far too close together for my liking. They were impressed with the band and the reaction from the screaming fans. A record deal was on offer. But it was too late for me, as I was tired of it and couldn't muster any enthusiasm. I'd been listening to bands like Yes, Genesis, The Band, Led Zeppelin and Little Feat. I'd visit my friend Eric Cloughley and we'd get stoned listening to the music that we loved. I wanted to be in a band that was creating music similar to what I was listening to. It was a million miles away from anything related to The Rollers. My head was out of it and I honestly thought I'd rather have no success than be a successful Roller. I either had to bow out then or go all the way with it, so I chose to leave.

Tam didn't make it easy for me, as he really wanted me to stay and he kept appearing at the house telling me how silly I was being and that I was losing out on a golden opportunity of success. I eventually got my mother to answer the door and tell him I wasn't at home. He was right about The Rollers, though. I knew the guys would have success and I wished them well, but they all took it badly when I left them. They just dumped my gear at the door, rang the bell and ran off. But with hindsight, I realise that I made the right move, my life would be very different now if I'd stayed, but if Pilot hadn't happened, I might have ended up regretting the decision to leave The Rollers. Life can be a puzzle, but gut feelings can't be ignored.

Above: Christyan rehearsing at Craighall in 1971. L to R: Dougie Cochrane, Jake Dourley, Ronnie Hogg, David Paton. (*David Paton Collection*)

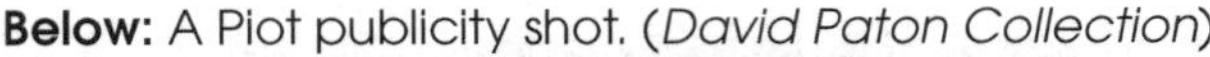

Below: A Piot publicity shot. (*David Paton Collection*)

Pilot

1970 to 1972. Fresh, Christyan and Craighall

Word got out that I had left the Rollers and I received a call from Dougie Cochrane from the group Tandem. I knew Dougie and Jake Dourley from The Inch housing estate. We were not great pals; there was just a polite 'hi there' when we saw each other. Dougie asked me if I'd be interested in forming a band with him and Jake to play more adventurous music and include some of our own compositions. Now I'm not a great believer in coincidence, but I do believe that sometimes things just fall into place; I can look back and see how one thing led to another and so on. I'm sure we all look back on circumstance and think, 'if I hadn't done this, then that would never have happened' or 'if I hadn't gone to that club, met that person, got on that bus, smoked that first cigarette, gone to the doctor'... It's endless; that's life.

A get-together was arranged with Dougie, Jake and myself. The talk was all about the music we enjoyed listening to and that we all wanted to play. I had an Island records sampler album which featured new signings to that label, and one of the bands on it was the band Free. I loved what I heard and I managed to get copies of their albums *Tons of Sobs* and *Fire and Water,* which had recently been released. 'Alright Now' had charted and Dougie and Jake were aware of that song. They loved the album when I played it to them, so we used Free as our role model. Our chat went well and we all agreed on the music we wanted to play and the direction we would take. We also noticed that Free were coming to Edinburgh, so we bought tickets for the gig and went along to see them. Wow! they were great. We were blown away and they were doing exactly what we wanted to do. Somebody came up with the name Fresh and we asked Tam Paton if he would look after us and get some gigs. He initially agreed, but he didn't like the direction we were going in and warned us that he'd find it hard to get us gigs if we didn't play popular chart songs. Tam still wanted me in The Rollers. He wanted Dougie too, and asked him if he could persuade me to give it another think-through. I told Dougie I'd made my final decision.

One problem was that Jake was a lead guitarist and so was I; one lead guitarist in a band is more than enough. Playing bass was something I really enjoyed, so I agreed to move onto bass and play just a couple of songs on lead guitar and I bought a Fender Precision bass at Clinkscales music shop in Galashiels.

Meanwhile, Jake enjoyed writing his own songs and I was starting to dabble in this myself. But we did find it hard getting gigs and were only offered a few each month. Ronnie Hogg joined us on drums and helped to introduce Dougie and Jake to the joys of smoking hash. It wasn't long before we were all getting stoned on a regular basis and spent a lot of the time just laughing at everything.

One evening we were stopped by the police on a routine car stop. The officer did the usual 'evening lads, can I ask if you've been drinking tonight', he was shining a torch on our faces and from the back seat, Jake mumbled 'put that fuckin' light oot', we burst out laughing. Luckily the officer didn't hear him or even realise we were all stoned, or we could all have been arrested.

The band all gathered at Jake's house for a meeting. He'd been sleeping and was a bit groggy. We decided that Jake would drive us into town and we could continue our meeting in the pub. I was sitting in the back of the car with an acoustic guitar playing and singing the Beatles song 'Bungalow Bill' as we drove up Minto Street towards the Newington area of the city. I could see the bus in front of us had stopped at a bus stop, but Jake didn't notice, so we smashed straight into the back of the stationary vehicle. Jake was knocked unconscious and Dougie sprang from the car holding his leg. I was saved from harm by my guitar, which took the full impact. Jake came round after ten minutes or so and Dougie recovered well, but it gave us all a fright.

We played regularly at the Dalkeith Arms. It's there that Ian Bairnson started to attend our gigs. I'd seen him play with the band East West a few times and he stood out as a fine player. He would come along to hear us play in Dalkeith and we'd sometimes invite him up for a couple of songs, including 'Alright Now'. I'm sure he liked us because we were not the run-of-the-mill chart covers band and were trying to do something different.

My sister was living in Edinburgh in a council flat with her husband Stuart, but they wanted to move back to London. Mary and I needed a flat and we wrote to the council to ask if we would be eligible to take over the flat my sister had. They agreed and the flat became ours when my sister and Stuart moved out.

Mary and I married on April 18 1972, after five years (on and off) of going together. I had been in London for a while and we split up, but we always got back together again and it was time to make a proper commitment. I realised how much she meant to me and I decided that I wanted to be with her permanently. One night we had been at a club and a guy asked her to dance. I watched them dancing and I thought 'she's my girl'. It must have been jealousy, but I walked over to them and lifted her from the dance floor, pinned her against the wall and told her then that I wanted to marry her.

I don't think we had many possessions at that time. Mary had been living in a rented flat in Stockbridge and I had moved in with her for a short spell, so it was just a case of buying bits and pieces that we needed to set up a home together. We did manage to buy some stuff, a piano and washing machine, from the auction rooms round the corner. With a little help from my friends, we managed to get the piano up a flight of stairs and into a tiny box room just off the living room. This is where I would spend most of my days writing music. Mary reminds me now that she helped me carry that washing machine, which would have been in September 1973 because she was eight months pregnant with Sarah at that time.

Fresh were up and running and self-indulgently, we were playing the kind of music we wanted to play. Our own compositions were included in the set, but sadly, we were not getting the same level of gigs as we did when we were with our former bands. Although we were enthusiastic and rehearsed almost every week, I think we enjoyed the music we played more than the punters did.

I had lost all contact with Billy Lyall, but I continued going to the music library and one day, I bumped into him as I was arriving and he was leaving. We met at the main entrance and he seemed embarrassed to see me. He was blushing and initially, he mumbled with his head down as we started chatting. It was raining as we stood in the doorway and caught up on what each of us had been up to in the last year. The significance of that meeting is discussed in a song I wrote called 'The Library Door' which is featured on the Pilot album *Two's a Crowd*. I tried to describe that meeting in the song, as it really was the birth of Pilot, so very important for both of us.

I was not aware at that time that Billy was gay. He'd never disclosed it to me and it wasn't something that was obvious so perhaps that explains the reason for his awkwardness. I told him I was playing bass with Fresh, writing songs and gigging. He said he finished with The Rollers shortly after I left and was now working at Craighall Studios as a sound engineer. Craighall was a subsidiary of EMI and as well as recording many Scottish artists such as Andy Stewart, Kenneth McKellar and Jimmy Shand, they also recorded the Edinburgh Military Tattoo and managed to have an LP of the performance in the shops before the end of the Edinburgh Festival. Many local bands had recorded in Craighall, including The Hipple People, The Moonrakers, The Avengers and The Athenians. Established in 1961, the studio had the first Neve 8058 to be installed in a UK studio, an analogue console that consists of 24 channels. Ask any experienced engineer or producer the question, 'if there was only one desk you could work on, what would it be?' and the overwhelming answer would be a Neve.

Billy and I talked about getting together and he said he could arrange studio time to record original songs on a regular basis. He lived at 6 Tarvit Street in Tollcross, just a short walk from where Mary and I lived at 6 Glen Street and he invited me down to see the studio the next week.

I was really knocked out by Craighall. It was such a professional studio and the lay out was just perfect. Billy played me a few of the songs he had written and recorded. Amazingly, he handled the recording, playing and singing all on his own. He explained that he had to start the multitrack in 'record', then run from the control room, open and close two heavy soundproof doors, and then get settled in front of the microphone with headphones on, before the track started. When he played the tracks to me, I could hear him running from the control room, then the studio door closing behind him.

But his songs were really good. He wrote quirky material with really interesting chord progressions and the subject matter was pretty 'out there' too, with titles like 'Alexander', 'King of Cancer', 'Mainline Expression', and 'Auntie Iris'. Yeah, he was inventive. I thought to myself that he had a little gold mine here and I was really looking forward to working with someone that I felt really compatible with – someone I respected musically – someone creative. We'd both worked together with The Rollers for a year or so but never really had a chance to show how creative we could be, so working together in Craighall Studios was going to be a great opportunity. It was just the right kind of motivation for me to put more time into writing songs. We arranged a date to start recording and I left Craighall feeling very excited about the prospect of working with Billy.

Pilot. Craighall 1972 and 1973

A week later, I arrived at the studio armed with my Fender Precision, a Spanish guitar and an electric. We got to work straight away. Early recordings were very experimental, and I remember that at one point, we both decided to write a song about our time with The Rollers. I wrote 'Mr Tam Bam' and Billy wrote 'Lost In Your Dreams'. I still have the recordings, although as the lyrics are a little negative, I'd prefer them not to be part of the Pilot legacy.

While Billy and I were busy and engrossed in our writing and recording, Fresh somehow managed to obtain a record deal with Decca Records. That contact might have come via Craighall – I don't remember. Apparently, there was another band with the name Fresh, so we changed our name to Christyan. We recorded the track 'Nursery Lane' written by Jake, which was a good song and was produced by Ray Horricks at Craighall. Billy engineered and played piano on the recording. We picked up a few plays on Radio One and the song was well-liked, but it didn't quite capture the imagination of the general public.

Meanwhile, both Bryce Laing (the owner and studio manager at Craighall studios) and Billy were very helpful to me and offered me session work as a bass player and guitarist. Bryce also allowed Billy and me to use the downtime at the studio to record whenever it wasn't booked out.

I was still with Christyan when I got the idea for the song 'Magic'.

When I composed on a piano, I'd have my cassette recorder sitting on top and I'd record any ideas that came into my head. Even if it was just four bars, I'd record it. The 'Magic' chorus was one of those four bar ideas that I liked – I was just waiting for the right verse to pop into my head. It's strange that 'Magic' is really just that – a four-bar chorus repeated. The verse is the same. It's a very simple format with some complicated chord progressions, and it's the most successful song I've ever written.

The idea for the verse came when I had to get up very early one morning to deliver milk for a local dairy owned by a friend. The sun was just coming up as I was dressing when Mary said to me, 'I've never been awake to see the day break'. I heard her words as a melody and I knew they would fit with my 'Magic' chorus. But it was too early in the morning to sit at the piano in the flat, so I wrote the melody down on a piece of music paper together with the chords I could visualise in my head: G...Bm...Em9...Am... Cø7...C...D and so on. I pieced it together after I had finished the milk round and could hear the arrangement, complete with the hand claps and the 'la la la's'. All of it was in my head. I was no more excited about writing 'Magic' than I was about most of the songs I was writing at the time. It was another song idea that would be recorded in Craighall.

But when we did start recording it, the song started to stand out; the demo sounded great. I knew there would be a guitar solo and I worked it out in the studio. In fact, all the important parts of the arrangement just came together without too much of a struggle. Billy added flute to the second half of the chorus and that was a really nice touch. The flute and the handclaps really lift it and the demo sounded great.

I let Christyan hear the recording and we included the song in our set with Dougie singing it. We were beginning to include more of our own songs in the setlist, but all was not going well with gigs and we all knew that we were reaching the end of our time as a band. My main thoughts were really on the writing and recording now and the studio work with Billy became the most important place for all my musical ideas

As gigs dried up for Christyan, The Rollers were starting to have nationwide success, so Tam put all his energies into the one camp and Christyan just quietly folded.

I was offered the gig as the resident bass player with The Band of Gold, which I took. They played five nights a week at the Mecca-owned Tiffany's, in Stockbridge. Ian Bairnson played guitar with the band, and of course, he was already held in high regard because of his accomplished playing. At that time, he was madly in love with Marilyn, the female singer in the band and they kept themselves apart from the other members of the group. During breaks, they'd disappear into the dressing room while the band went to the bar. I have to say that Ian was extremely frugal. He'd never be seen at the bar buying a round of drinks. Frugality can develop into a kind of penny-pinching illness with some folk, which is a weakness and can be a bit tiresome.

'Magic' was included in the set with The Band of Gold. The regulars got to know it was my song. One evening during our break, I was approached by a guy who started asking me questions about it. I told him I hadn't long written it and it was one of many original compositions. He said he'd like to buy the song from me and offered £200, which was a month's wages at that time. But I knew I had written a good song and it was very popular, so I certainly wasn't going to sell it to anyone.

Meanwhile, the recordings continued at Craighall, but we really needed a drummer.

In February 1973, Mary told me I was going to be a dad. A dad! Fantastic! I don't know how we managed to cope in a one-bedroom flat with no bath, but there was a good feeling in the flat and we had many evenings with friends chatting and listening to music. Luckily, my Mum and Dad lived in the next street, so we were free to pop round there any time for a bath or shower.

I continued the process of trying to perfect my songwriting. Billy would drop by every so often and we'd arrange studio dates for recording or take a trip to the library for more music to play together. We did spend a lot of time listening to and playing music together. Elton John was a big favourite and we loved his album *Madman Across The Water*. We also attended a few concerts. Being the bass player at a Mecca venue, I was always getting tickets to see some great bands, including Free, The Who, Sweet and Slade. As we were both interested in classical music, Billy would arrange tickets for concerts. I remember he arranged tickets to attend a performance of Mozart's *The Magic Flute*. That was the first classical concert I'd been to, and I loved it.

We took our music very seriously and the studio time was really well appreciated and treated with respect. Although it was relaxed, we had work to do and we'd become totally absorbed in it. We could usually complete a song from Billy and a song of mine on the same night. If we got our heads down, we got the work done with no distractions. It was a kind of mission and as a rule, we didn't invite friends down unless they were working with us. Mary came along to the studio a couple of times but soon got bored with the process of recording as she preferred to hear the finished songs rather than sit through hours of hearing the same piece over and over. Nobby Clark from The Rollers remained a good friend of both Billy and I, and he helped out with backing vocals on a couple of songs, but it was generally just Billy and me working together.

Life was settling down and there was a pattern evolving with the writing improving with every song. I loved Billy's writing; it was clever and witty. Playing bass and following what he played on piano with his left hand was always fun and his chord structures fascinated me. By comparison, my songs were a lot more straightforward; or so I thought.

The Band of Gold had a stand-in drummer (a dep) by the name of Stuart Tosh. With no disrespect to the regular guy, Stuart was a proper rock drummer. The drums were on a riser (a raised platform) on the stage at Tiffany's, so I generally stood in front of the drum kit on stage. When Stuart took the drum stool, I was aware of the thump of the bass drum and there was a rush of air that hit me in the back every time his foot pedal hit the drum. Stuart learned to play 'Magic' and was very enthusiastic about the song. He kept telling me it was a hit and that I should get it to a record company. I told him about Billy and I working together and invited him down to Craighall to play some drums for us. He was very happy to get involved and on our first recordings with Stuart, we realised we'd found the missing element that was really needed to help lift the overall presentation of the songs. The demos took on a new life and our excitement was growing with every recording we made as a trio.

Stuart put in many hours work on the songs, which was very nice of him as there was no financial reward at that stage. In fact, he was probably more enthusiastic than Billy and I. He was so keen that he'd be knocking on my door in Glen Street at 10 am, asking Mary if he could talk to me. He just wanted to talk about the songs and couldn't get them out of his head. Billy was writing great songs, too and together, we really had managed to create a distinctive sound and a good collection of tracks. With Stuart now on board, it was even better; the writing, the playing and Billy's production and engineering were superb. A few of the songs were re-recorded with drums and it was then that we knew there was really something to shout about.

Stuart recalled to me: 'I always thought Craighall had a perfect room sound and brightness for rock n roll. There was a fresh sound in all our demos and sometimes I wonder, how would an album have sounded, had we recorded one there'.

We wanted a guitar player to help out in case we did some live work. Billy mentioned a guy named Les Davidson. I asked Billy to make contact with him and invite him down to play on a track or two. He played guitar on a song of Billy's called 'Love Has Got Me By The Throat'. He played really well and we asked him to join us. He said he liked the music and enjoyed working with us, but he turned us down, saying he wanted to get into Jazz a bit more. That was disappointing for us because we thought that his playing and personality worked well for us. Les went on to have a very successful career as a session player. He has worked with East of Eden, Rumer, Joan Armatrading, Donovan, Pete Townsend, Tina Turner and Bill Wyman. We met up again in the late 80s, and he told me he wished he'd taken the offer to be with us, but I don't think he had any regrets, really. I asked Ian Bairnson along to the studio to play on Billy's song 'Just Let Me Be'. He played really well, but as he was intending to move down to London to pursue his own career, we didn't ask if he'd like to join us permanently.

So, as Les and Ian were not available to join us, we decided to carry on recording as a three-piece. I would play guitar and bass on the songs for now. But Stuart said he had a friend at EMI, an old school pal named John Cavanagh. He managed to contact John and he asked Stuart if we could come down to London and have a meeting with him. Billy and I liked this idea and asked Stuart to set it up.

It was early September 1973. The meeting with John was arranged at EMI records, Manchester Square, London. We booked a sleeper train to London which would arrive very early morning at Kings Cross. As Mary was heavily pregnant and the baby was due within a couple of weeks, it was a bit risky. But she was being looked after, so I agreed to the meeting and hoped everything would work out well.

Billy, Stuart and I set off on the overnight train from Waverley station Edinburgh. Can you imagine trying to sleep on a train knowing you're meeting with The Beatles' record company in the morning? We arrived at Kings Cross bleary-eyed in the early hours. Somehow, we got lost on the way to Manchester square, but after asking for directions, we made it, and as we were early we had a bit of breakfast before the meeting.

We nervously arrived and were met in reception by John's secretary, who took us to his office. Stuart recalls. 'I remember in the reception area, we looked up and realised that was the location where the photograph of The Beatles looking down over the staircase was taken for the *Please Please Me* album.

There were the usual introductions and another cup of tea. But John was keen to hear the music and we were keen to play it to him. Billy had the masters on a quarter-inch tape which was a standard format at that time. John threaded the tape onto the Teac recorder. He turned the dial and within a few seconds, the room filled with the sound of Pilot. As he listened, his eyes lit up, 'oh I like this, guys. I'd like to play this to another label manager, do you mind?' he said. He disappeared to another office and returned with a colleague. As he was to become a significant but controversial figure over the next few years, we'll call him 'Dim' to protect his real identity.

We were introduced and played a couple of songs again. Dim thought the songs were excellent and suggested that we should meet with the head of A&R, Roy Featherstone. As we had booked the return train for that evening, a meeting was quickly set up for that afternoon. We headed off to the pub and discussed our good fortune at receiving such a positive response from John and Dim. John joined us in the pub and told us we really had something special. I was overcome by this – I think we all were – we just didn't expect such an enthusiastic response. It wasn't long before we were back at EMI meeting with Roy. He, too, couldn't hide his joy and enthusiasm for our music; he told us we had a deal and that we just needed to find ourselves a manager and lawyer to help negotiate for us. We returned to Edinburgh on the overnight train with really positive thoughts on things to come and, of course, another sleepless night.

Bryce Laine offered me some session work playing the guitar for a classical album consisting of music from the Baroque period. The request was made very formally with a letter detailing the times, the fee and the instruments required. I was a bit nervous about it, but with encouragement from Billy, I agreed to do the session. There was really no need for me to be nervous as the session went very well and I enjoyed playing with classical musicians and reading the guitar parts. Bryce asked me to do more sessions and I was happy to oblige. In 2020 I found a letter from Bryce requesting me as a bass player on a session for October 1 and 2, 1973 – just two days before my daughter Sarah was born. I remember those events very well. Mary was admitted into hospital in the early morning. She was in labour for a long time but Sarah was born on October 4, 1973. I stayed with Mary at the hospital all day until I was told to leave after the birth at around 8.30 pm. I went straight to the gig at Tiffany's an hour late and was presented with a bottle of champagne on stage. I felt good – almost like a grown-up!

The next day we had to be in London for more dealings with EMI. In the 1970s, they kept the mum and baby in hospital for a couple of days after the birth, so I felt that I could disappear for the day and be back the following morning to collect Mary and Sarah.

The band were beginning to see signs of the star treatment now. EMI were booking flights and a hotel for our overnight stays and picking up the tab. We had a meeting with EMI and then a chat with John and Dim. We flew back the next day, and I went straight to the hospital to pick up Mary and our beautiful baby daughter.

However, my car was a Capri Classic; a Ford, not in great condition but quite a rare car. It wouldn't start when I jumped into it at the airport. I raised the bonnet and checked the distributor cap. It was wet, so I dried it off, checked the carburettor and turned the key. It still wouldn't start. I removed the plugs and cleaned them with a wire brush that I kept in the boot, as issues with the car weren't out of the ordinary for me. I turned the key. It started, but my hands were covered in oil. When I got to the hospital, I was a bit late and rushed upstairs to meet Mary with hands in my pockets – a kiss but no cuddle. OK, I was in a bit of a mess and looked like a mechanic, but at least I was there and only ten minutes late.

In those days, a nurse carried the baby to the car. Sarah was placed on Mary's lap in the front seat and we set off home, but the car door didn't close properly and Mary had to hold it shut with one hand and keep a grip on Sarah with the other. You wouldn't get away with that now. I was starving and I stopped for a fish supper on the way back.

But disaster! There was no music in the car. My daughter had to hear music and quickly, so Sarah heard The Beatles and Beethoven as soon as we arrived home. Even though I really was a bit of a yob in those days, I learned fathership as I went along.

I went back to Tiffany's the next night and Dougie Cochrane, who was now singing with The Band of Gold, told me I'd better tell the boss I was leaving because I was about to get sacked for taking too much time off. I realised that I couldn't continue with the house band as events in London were becoming more demanding. I spoke to the boss and said it was probably better for me to finish as soon as they found a replacement. That was the end of Tiffany's for me and the beginning of a fast-paced life that was about to knock me flying.

On our next trip to London, Dim asked us if we'd meet with his brother, who worked for EMI publishing at offices that were not far from Manchester Square. Another trek to another office and the songs were played to… well, I'll call him 'Thick', (trench coat, blonde hair, small round glasses and eyes too close together for my liking, does that sound familiar?). The brothers informed us that they had all the inside knowledge needed to help secure a good deal with EMI and that they could advise us and keep us right in many areas. They were offering to manage us. It seemed to make sense to have them involved as we needed someone in the know and quickly. I had my reservations and that gut feeling again that all wasn't entirely well, but I put it to the back of my mind. With hindsight, I realise the mistakes we made. It would have been a conflict of interest to have them sign us to EMI as they already worked there, so they resigned from their jobs and so initially Thick and Dim, with John Cavanagh, managed Pilot. To his credit, John dropped out of the management agreement and continued as an EMI employee.

A management contract was presented to us and we signed totally and naively, trusting them to be fair, which was a big mistake. We didn't even consult a lawyer about the contract we signed. Instead, we went to their lawyer, who read through the clauses and explained everything. For all you budding musicians out there, always have your own lawyer check your contracts, no matter what you're told.

There was no name for the band at that time, but a clever girlfriend of someone in the management came up with the idea of using the initials of our surnames Paton, Lyall, Tosh, and the name PiLoT was created from that.

I had set myself goals, but I never expected to get this far, as initially, I only wanted to be able to play the guitar, and then I wanted to play with a band. Then a day in a studio was an early goal, then writing a half-decent song, then playing regular gigs, and making a record. But it was all happening like a hurricane now. We had all the pieces of the jigsaw.

The ball was really rolling for us, the EMI contract was signed, and Abbey Road Studio Two was booked for us. We were given a list of in-house engineers and asked to pick one. There were ten names on the list and I knew a few of them. One name, in particular, stood out – Alan Parsons. I knew that name from Pink Floyd's *Dark Side of the Moon* and a couple of Beatles and McCartney albums. Billy agreed that we should give him a try. Alan was ready to graduate from engineering to producing, so he was invited up to Craighall and we put him on the spot by asking him to mix a couple of our songs. He was a little reluctant, but he did a mix and he made a great job of it.

Alan is a giant. He is 6 feet 4 inches, from a Scottish mother and English father. He came from public schooling and was very much a gentleman. He was really good at his job, so we couldn't have picked a better producer, but he was quiet, reserved and only spoke when necessary. You could sit for hours with him on a mix, and after a while, he'd ask, 'any thoughts?' We'd always answer, 'No, Alan, it sounds great', and it did. Very rarely, if ever, did we have any negative comments about the mixes, as he heard the music in exactly the same way that we did.

1974. Abbey Road and success!

My God, this was heaven for a musician and I was so excited.

The Beatles meant everything to me and here I was in their workshop and about to record my own music, using the same mics, pianos, congas, seats, floor, bannister, toilets and canteen. We even had the use of the Mellotron they used on 'Strawberry Fields Forever'. We had the run of the place and it soon felt like home. The canteen was used by us every day. The food tasted good and was prepared well considering it was just an ordinary canteen at that time.

We arrived for lunch one day and Stuart noticed steak on the menu. When it was his turn to be served, he said to Doris, the canteen lady, in his poshest Aberdeen accent: 'I'll have a Sirloin steak please, and I'd like it medium'. In a broad cockney accent, Doris replied, 'Oh they're all the same size, dear'. Doris even arranged to have Haggis on the menu for Burns Night, bless her. We used one of these ladies on an Alan Parsons Project instrumental called 'Hawkeye', from the 1985 *Vulture Culture* album. You can hear her say 'only what's on the menu' with a thick Caribbean accent.

So here we were, in Abbey Road. We set up very quickly and got into the swing of it. Everything we needed was on hand or could be hired and delivered within a couple of hours. I hired a Rickenbacker 480 guitar and we started work on the first song, 'Just a Smile'. I don't want to get too technical, but I did lay down four Rickenbacker guitar parts, two acoustics and bass guitar. With Stuart on drums and Billy on piano and Hammond organ, the sound in the control room was awesome. By the time the vocals and handclaps went down, we were all ecstatic. We kept saying to Alan, play it again, play it again. We wanted to hear it over and over, and I think Alan did too. But the rest of the songs were recorded in a more relaxed way. We wanted a good drum track, as dropping in a late snare or cymbal crash would be pretty difficult, so a good drum track is what we aimed for with all the songs, and everything else could be overdubbed or replaced if necessary. We added embellishments to each song, but 'Just a Smile' had the biggest impact on me because it was the first song we recorded, and I'll never forget the feeling of hearing it played back to us. It was majestic, the sound of Pilot – distinctive and unique.

Ian Bairnson had played on one of Billy's songs at Craighall in Edinburgh called 'Just Let Me Be'. We wanted to re-record the song as a B-side and decided to ask Ian along to play on it. We knew where he was – he'd left Tiffany's in Edinburgh and was now gigging in a Tiffany's in London. We went to see him play with the house band – it was the same gig in a different city. He jumped at the invitation to play guitar for us, the session went well and the guitar part was exactly what we wanted to hear. Ian is such a refined guitar player, a true natural and very particular about what he plays. If he wasn't happy, if there was one tiny flaw (that's hardly noticeable), he'd want to do it again. He enjoyed being in Abbey Road and asked if he could come on by again. I told him he was welcome anytime.

When it came to the mixing of the album, Alan spent a lot of time setting up and the band got around to talking about performing live. We needed another member and as I was thinking of playing guitar rather than bass, Ian didn't immediately spring to mind. I always thought Ian would want to pursue a different path and playing in a pop band didn't seem to be on his list. I auditioned a few bass players in the studio while Alan was mixing in the control room, but I didn't think any of them were right for Pilot. For whatever reason, they just didn't fit. I wanted someone who played bass in the way that I played – someone with a Paul McCartney influence – so I was very particular. I then turned my attention to trying out a few guitar players. I didn't ask Ian to the auditions, although he had started to drop by on a regular basis and he would sit in the control room with Alan and listen to the mixing sessions. I think he liked what he heard. In fact, Ian did drop in while I was busy with auditions and I could see him chatting to Alan.

Things were not going well with guitar player auditions. It was tiresome and frustrating, so I went up to the control room for a break and a coffee. Ian asked me what was going on and I told him I was at the end of my tether with guitar players. 'Why didn't you ask me?' he said. Well, I had thought about it by then and had mentioned it to a couple of people, but the response was negative. 'He doesn't look the part,' was the reply. I didn't understand. 'He doesn't look the part?' How ridiculous; he played like a world-class musician. EMI were particularly vocal about this as the 'teenybop' band thing was huge in the UK then, and perhaps they thought they could capitalise on that with us. Billy and I had even grown moustaches at that time, as a kind of rebellion against that. There's no way I wanted to be labelled a teenybop band, so I told Ian if he wanted the gig, it was his. Stuart and Billy both agreed that he was a superior guitar player and head and shoulders above any of the others we'd listened to. I'd had enough of auditions and I'd had enough of EMI wanting to promote us as lightweights. I took a lot of flak for insisting that Ian play the guitar, but we were more than a bubble-gum band and I didn't want EMI to promote us in that way. 'Nip it in the bud now', I thought. Ian did help bring more credibility to the band and that's exactly why I wanted him there. We really gelled in the studio and during live performances and Ian's guitar playing became an integral part of the Pilot sound, so I am certain that we made the right decision by standing our ground.

We decided to add another track to the first album and we chose a Billy Lyall composition called 'High Into The Sky'. This was a perfect opportunity to have Ian play along with us. We really gelled as a unit in the studio and felt confident about doing live performances. Recording with Ian worked perfectly and we felt confident we could tour with this line-up.

Pilot, Queen and Cockney Rebel would spearhead the launch of a new label for EMI just called 'EMI' and as a friendly gesture, they arranged a dinner for Queen and Pilot just so that we could chat and get to know one another. The dinner went well and we got on great with Queen. It was obvious to me that Freddie Mercury wanted to be a star and nothing else seemed to matter. He was totally immersed in his writing, his band, ambitions and dreams. I suppose we all were, but it was particularly noticeable with Freddie.

EMI asked us to perform our debut gig at an EMI conference in the Gleneagles Hotel, Perthshire. Although it was pretty nerve-racking, we were delighted to stand up in front of high flyers in the music industry and let them hear what we could do. The gig was great and we received many congratulations and voices of support for our upcoming releases. It also seemed quite appropriate that we performed our very first gig as a band in Scotland.

Billy and I never actually wrote songs together, but we agreed to name all the songs for the first album Paton/Lyall compositions in the Lennon/McCartney style.

We came up with a quirky album title *From the Album of the Same Name* and when all the recordings were completed, we had a playback for EMI in Abbey Road. They seemed to genuinely love what they heard and suggested adding orchestration to the singles. Oh dear, how original. When they couldn't think of anything to say but wanted to add input, they often said, you need a string section, as it made them think that they sounded like they knew what they were talking about. However, we found it very predictable. Still, it was going to be at our expense in the long run, so the string section was booked for a day in Abbey Road. It was also suggested that we have a more dynamic introduction for 'Magic'. The original recording starts with the chorus, just piano and voice. Although I play the guitar throughout the song, we asked Ian to join us for the rerecording of the new and more dynamic intro. Andrew Powell did a great job of arranging and conducting and it was a novelty to hear our songs with a string arrangement, but I still don't think you can turn a song into a hit just by adding strings. It was a fashion – the thing to do at the time – and to be honest, I still prefer the album version of 'Just A Smile' without strings. We had a final mix and playback, which took us to 5 am on the final day, and the band drifted in and out of sleep during the final mixing. Alan did a fantastic job and we felt elated as we walked out of the studio and into the daylight and the dawn chorus, exhausted, delighted and excited about our debut album.

The recordings were over for now and I flew back home for a few days rest. This is not easy when your head is full of thoughts on things to come and the telephone never stopped ringing. The wheels were in motion and there were photo shoots, interviews and a tour being arranged.

I'm an obsessive person, but I felt like I was missing out on seeing Mary and Sarah while my dreams were being fulfilled. I realised I was missing out on quality family time. That's a dilemma that needs a lot of careful thought, but I was given all the support I needed by Mary and she encouraged me to go for it all the way.

We were given the opportunity to support Sparks on their upcoming tour of the UK. 'Just A Smile' was released as our first single but only made a minor impression. However, the reviews were great and DJ Annie Nightingale's comment, 'whoever wrote this must surely have a long career ahead in music' thrilled me to pieces. 'Magic' was scheduled for release to coincide with the Sparks tour. This is when we really stared to see things happen. Halfway into the tour, 'Magic' charted and the concert dates began selling out everywhere. We really enjoyed the tour, although Billy had a hard time keeping his ARP synthesisers in tune – it drove him crazy. Synthesisers were in their infancy then and caused a lot of frustration on the road. The oscillators had a habit of drifting out and they had to be manually tuned for almost every song. With Billy being such a perfectionist, he became exasperated at this, so he'd come off stage and throw a tantrum. Bottles would be hurled against walls and he'd pace up and down, swearing and red in the face with anger. We all felt for him, but he just had to make the best of it. The Sparks guys were good company, although the Mael brothers kept themselves locked up in their hotel room a lot of the time.

Occupying your time on the road can be a bit difficult. We seemed to spend hours throwing Frisbees back and forward to each other. After breakfast, before shows, during sound checks, a Frisbee was a kind of mascot to us. Playing concert halls and theatres was a real treat and amassing more and more Pilot fans was fantastic and made the concerts so much more enjoyable. Now that 'Magic' had charted, we weren't just supporting Sparks, but people were buying tickets to see Pilot.

We were out on the road and adapting to the life fairly well. Stuart Tosh told me that even though this is the career we strived for and that this was the dream, now that it was happening, he felt numb. We all did. The tour became a whirlwind of concerts, interviews and meetings with so-called 'important people' – whatever that means.

I had a strange coincidence with numbers on tour with Pilot. I booked into the De Vere Hotel, Coventry 11.11.1974, where my room number was 505. This was fine, there was nothing unusual about that. The next night was The Royal Lancaster, London, room 505. Hmm, that's the same number I had last night. On the 13th, it was the Dragon Hotel Swansea, room 505. Three consecutive nights with the same room number. I kept the check-in cards and put them in my Pilot scrapbook. 505 does seem to be a significant number in my life and I'm reminded of it from time to time. It might be waking up three consecutive mornings at 5:05 am or maybe it'll be there on a receipt for coffee and a bun. It's there more often than just coincidence.

I googled 505 and this is what I read: 'Your guardian angels are sending you this number as a reminder that you need to make changes, and the sooner you do it, the better! You may notice that you see this number everywhere, so frequently that it feels like this number is stalking you'.

But in the months to come, I would begin to realise that I really did need to make changes. With the tour at an end, another ambition that I thought was beyond reach was fulfilled with an appearance on *Top of the Pops*, the first of many, and a song in the charts. It wasn't just *TOTP*. It was *Supersonic*, *Blue Peter* and *Magpie* – kid's TV shows in the UK – and we were flying back and forward to Europe to do the same thing there. We had many TV and radio dates in the diary, the EMI publicity machine was giving us a big push and we had to make ourselves available for any opportunity to publicise the band.

It was time to think about writing a second album. Songs were spilling from me and it seemed that every time I sat at the piano, I created another one. Mary was responsible for the inspiration behind 'January'. She was reading a book and I asked her if it was good and what it was about. She said it was terrific and that the name of the heroine was January. She thought it was an unusual name and I thought about other months that were used as girls' names; April, May and June have all been used, but January did seem a little unusual. The next time I sat down at the piano, 'January' just popped into my head. The verse came a few days later and was pretty much unrelated to the chorus.

Life gets me higher,
I can show, I can glow,
I can wake up the world,
little world,
gotta know you, gotta show you.

So, it must have been mid-November and very shortly after the tour and success of 'Magic' that Stuart, Billy and I were back in Craighall recording demos for a second album. It was great fun, we were on a high, and you can hear it in the demos. Our faces were becoming well known, and that has a downside, as my social life suffered badly. I wanted to go to the pub with my mates or to a restaurant or the cinema with Mary, but even going shopping was stressful. It was fine at first, but I began to dislike the attention I was receiving. What a dilemma. From the day I picked up a guitar, I wanted to be a successful musician, but I didn't enjoy being famous or in the spotlight – it's my Achilles heel. When I watch the *X Factor* on TV now, I realise what lengths some people will go to just to be famous, although the funny thing is that I get wrapped up in it and really feel for them.

We started recording the second album in late 1974 at George Martin's Air Studios, Oxford Circus. 'January' was recorded first as it was an obvious contender for a single and we wanted it out for January 1975. On release, it didn't take long to start climbing the charts.

While recording the *Second Flight* album, I stayed for a couple of nights with my sister in Bromley, Kent. I set off for the studio on the morning of the announcement of the new chart positions. My hire car didn't have a radio in it, so I was unaware of the chart position of 'January'. As I walked into the reception of the studio, Alan was there to meet me, he held out his hand and said, 'Congratulations, David, 'January' is number one'. 'Oh my God, I've written a UK number one chart song'. It was that feeling of disbelief that you get with good news or bad news. 'No, it can't be true, there must be some mistake, this is not really happening'. The studio was just a buzz of excitement. I had to speak to Mary to hear if she knew. She knew, alright; her younger sister was coming to the flat for lunch and the chart positions on the radio chart show had reached number two without mention of Pilot. She was hanging out the window, telling Linda to leg it up the stair before the number one was announced. They jumped up and down and cried with joy when they heard the DJ announce, 'and this week at Number one is Pilot', she was still crying when I spoke to her.

We were back on the rollercoaster again, with everyone wanting a piece of Pilot. I was standing on set at *Top Of The Pops,* waiting for the cameras to roll, when a girl in the audience spoke to me. She offered her congratulations and she asked, 'You look really happy; how does it feel to be number one?'. I told her that I felt like I was on top of the world, so lucky, privileged, overwhelmed, bursting with the excitement of it all, a dream fulfilled. I suppose being where I was, on set, at the top of the chart, I did think, 'Yeeessss I've done it, and I'm still not quite believing it, if I'm dreaming, I don't want to wake up'.

It was the most talked about and biggest-selling song in the country for the next three weeks. It was a fantastic moment. I had achieved a lifetime ambition and was pretty pleased with myself. We'd signed with EMI less than a year ago and here we were at number one. What a fantastic achievement.

The cameras rolled and we performed our song to finish the show. I wrote the song 'Trembling' about appearing on TV for the first time:

> I'm trembling head to my feet, Ooh I'm weak,
> hard shake up cool make up, cover this boy with light
> I'm changing my smile to a frown, cool me down.
> Now or never, forever, follow this boy around

Freddie Mercury

After the show was recorded, we made our way to the bar and I saw Freddie Mercury walk in with a minder. I spoke about the EMI launch with Michael Heatley:

> Let's wind the story back to 1974, when EMI – which, of course, had existed for many years – launched a new flagship label bearing the company name. The first three acts were Pilot, Queen and Cockney Rebel, and a friendly rivalry developed to get to number one. 'January' won, only to be deposed by Cockney Rebel's 'Make Me Smile (Come Up And See Me)'.
>
> Coming third in a three-horse race clearly upset Freddie Mercury, and a chance meeting with David at BBC-TV's *Top of the Pops* gave Queen's front man the chance to say so. 'He came in the bar after the show and I thought I'd say hello. We'd been for a couple of meals together; EMI wanted us to be friendly, and we'd chatted. He was totally obsessed, couldn't talk about anything else but himself and how he wanted to be famous. I went over and asked how he was doing. 'Congratulations on your number one,' he said. 'And, by the way, when *I'm* number one … (dramatic pause) …I won't be talking to you!" I have since found out from Martin Hutchison that Whispering Grass by Winsor Davies and Don Estelle was the 3rd number one on the new label'.

His sycophantic friend seemed to find that a very witty remark. It was actually a bit hurtful, but I realised that he wanted to be number one and was annoyed, maybe even angry, at us getting there before him. We had both signed to the new EMI label at the same time, but I didn't realise he was treating it as a competition to be the first to reach such a position on the new label.

Pilot problems

Billy decided to come out and announce that he was gay. That was OK, but he wasn't having an easy time coping with being in a successful group. His personality was changing and he became quite unpredictable sometimes. While Alan was mixing *Second Flight*, Billy decided that he didn't like one of the mixes and said he could do it better. This was slightly embarrassing and should have been discussed in private, not in front of Alan. But Billy had his own way of doing things. We knew Billy was an excellent engineer and as a result, if he had produced the band, he would have been much happier. He wasn't pleased that none of his songs were being released as singles, and when I wrote 'Call Me Round' and Ian added a middle eight, he wasn't happy about that either. Alan graciously did not protest about Billy wanting to do a mix and he allowed Billy to have a go. He probably spent an hour or so mixing, but he did have Alan's template and didn't really start the mix from scratch. When he finished, we all gathered in the control room and listened to it. It was good, it was very good, but I wouldn't say it was better than Alan's effort and it was an awkward situation. We had to be both diplomatic and truthful, which was not an easy task. We all agreed that we liked Alan's mix better, but there really wasn't a lot in it. Alan was there to produce the band and he was doing a great job of it. But Billy just handled the whole process in a very brash manner and It would have caused a major upset if we had allowed Billy to take over mixing at that stage.

Meanwhile, he was becoming more distant and increasingly involved with the gay scene in London. He was unhappy living in Edinburgh, and as he put it, 'I'm sick of being served my gin and tonic in a half pint glass with no ice or lemon'. He wanted the finer things in life and enjoyed the London lifestyle. Stuart moved south too, but I stayed put. I was very happy in Edinburgh.

We all went for a meal to celebrate our success. Billy got very drunk and fell asleep at the table, so Stuart had to prop him up and keep his hair out of his plate of soup. But at the restaurant, I couldn't eat the food that was served. I was having difficulty swallowing it and, in the end, just had water. As we were walking back from the restaurant, I felt my face go very hot – I couldn't explain it. When I got to the hotel, I had a shower and dried off, but when I looked in the mirror, my face was very red and burning hot. This was a bit worrying; what was going on? Initially, I thought I'd maybe picked up a virus, but it stayed with me, my condition didn't get any worse, but it didn't getting any better.

I started having trouble digesting food, especially meat. I visited my doctor and an appointment was made at the Edinburgh Royal Infirmary. I was examined, x-rayed and blood was taken. Then I was given a barium meal which was horrible, but nothing untoward was found. The condition stayed with me and I gave up eating meat completely, which helped. I realise now that this and the skin complaint were stress related. It could have been the stress of being in the public eye and not feeling comfortable with it. The condition carried on affecting me for a few months, although it did slowly ease as time went by. It's clear that too much was being asked of us and I wasn't able to deal with it mentally.

We started a second tour of the UK with Smokie in support. They were nice guys from Bradford, and we had fun together, even getting the guitars out for a singsong on occasion. It was fantastic to know there were so many people out there wanting to see and hear Pilot play; the gigs were great and it was – and remains – a real thrill to hear a packed audience sing along with you. I felt very at home gigging with Smokie and travelling around the UK and we'd sometimes sit in their bus with them just to chat during the journeys.

My skin condition was still with me and digesting food became really difficult. I was losing weight and my voice was suffering. High notes were not so easy to reach and I felt uncomfortable, as if there was something stuck in my throat. We were a little more than halfway through the tour when I realised I couldn't go on. I was taken to a doctor and given a tetanus shot for some reason – I never understood that one. I explained all my symptoms to the doctors, but they were at a loss to diagnose anything. The tour was cancelled, much to the disappointment of all concerned.

Second Flight was selling well and there was plenty of promotional work to do, so we kept busy.

It was all looking fantastic for Pilot except for one thing. What was happening to our earnings? The management bought themselves E-Type Jaguars, and then one of them appeared driving a Ferrari, which he was kind of showing off to us. Money was being advanced from EMI and the band were not being told about it. But our managers moved into plush offices in Knightsbridge. Meanwhile, I was living in a one-bedroom flat in Edinburgh, driving about in a clapped-out Ford. We were being paid salaries from the Pilot account, but the vast earnings that the band were generating were not coming our way. Something had to be done to rectify this. I remembered a clause in their contract that stated that management were entitled to 20% of our earnings plus reasonable expenses. This had gone well beyond reasonable. Here we were, living the dream, but I certainly wasn't happy. I seemed to be the only one who was suspicious that the big rewards for our success were not coming our way.

One day, I was sitting in the back of our manager's V12 2+2 E-type, his wife sitting up front beside him while I was squashed in the back. As we drove past a swanky Harrods-type store, she shouted, 'stop the car; I want that fur coat'. I couldn't believe what I was hearing. Thick was embarrassed and I was angry with her, not just at the request for a fur coat but also because I knew that I would probably be indirectly paying for something I consciously objected to, and all for the sake of her little whim. It felt like she was doing it on purpose to taunt me – taking the piss. I had to react. They may not have credited me with much intelligence, but they vastly underestimated my determination to rectify something that I thought to be underhand and unjust. I really felt I was being made a fool of.

It was time for me to be the precious rock star. Time to think about myself, be a little selfish, and a little unreasonable and start demanding a few things that I felt I had probably earned. Dim was driving me along the Old Kent Road in his E-type when I spotted another E-type on ramps on a garage forecourt. I said to him, 'stop the car, turn round, I want that car'. He replied, 'Don't be silly, David, you can't have that car'. But I said, 'Oh yes, I can. You have your fancy car and I'm driving about in a clapped-out Ford with the door falling off and it needs the plugs cleaned before the fuckin' thing will start. I wanted a decent car'. He relented and we drove back to look at it. It was a silver grey 4.2 drop head series two. It was beautiful. We spoke to the salesman and Dim handled the negotiations. After half an hour of haggling, the car was mine. Insurance was organised the same day and I drove back up to Edinburgh to surprise Mary. I parked the E-type outside the tenement in Glen Street. It looked slightly out of place, but wow, what a car, and it was mine. Not only was it a great-looking car, but it also turned out to be a really good investment. I had a Vespa scooter I used for buzzing about the town and a neighbour a few doors down also had a Vespa that was very troublesome, so I gave him mine and told him I wouldn't be needing it anymore. My classic, clapped-out Capri was given to a pal.

OK, I felt like I was getting somewhere now. I'd started my own little rebellion. The next thing I wanted to secure was a house. If I was going to squeeze anything out of them, I wanted it in bricks and mortar. I hear you saying 'spoiled bastard'. OK, but rightly or wrongly, I believed our earnings

Above: Taken in my studio for the *Magic Collection* CD in 2022. (*David Paton Collection*)

Right: On stage in an Edinburgh club with The Bay City Rollers 1970. (*David Paton Collection*)

Left: My mum Matilda Thomson and my dad, Jack Paton. This looks like a professional photograph from around 1944/45. *(David Paton Collection*)

Right: With my sister Ena (Nina). I look about five years old, and sis would have been eight. *(David Paton Collection*)

Left: This was on our journey to San Sebastian when I was 11 in 1960. We're in Parliament square. *(David Paton Collection*)

Right: At home with my mum around 1963. *(David Paton Collection)*

Left: With my dad in Blackpool. It must be around 1957 and I'd be eight years old. *(David Paton Collection)*

Left: The Beachcombers, 1968. Back: Sandy (bass), Kenny (drums). Front: me (guitar), Mike (vocals), Lex (organ). *(David Paton Collection*)

Above: The Beachcombers again. Sandy Walusiak, Kenny McLean, Mike Rowberry, Davie Anderson (rhythm guitar), and me. *(David Paton Collection*)

Left: The Bay City Rollers. Derek, Alan, me, Nobby and Billy in front (his favourite place).

Right: *From the Album of the Same Name*. Pilot's debut, which contained 'Magic', my best-known song. (*EMI*)

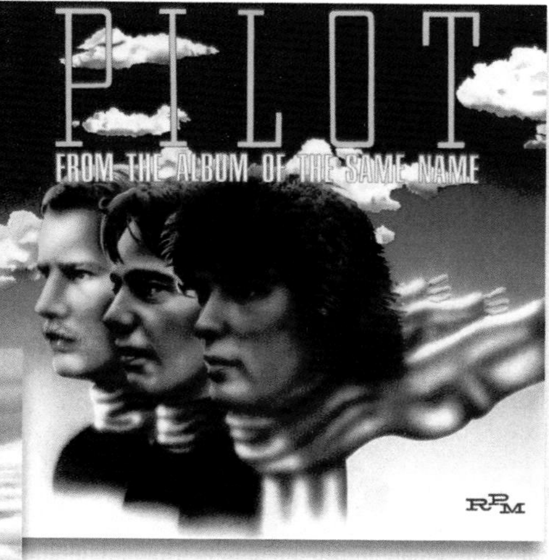

Below: *Second Flight*. Pilot's second album, which contained the UK and Australian number one, 'January'. (*EMI*)

Above: *Morin Heights*: Album number three from Pilot, recorded in Canada. (*EMI*)

Left: *Two's a Crowd*. The 1977 Pilot album featuring David Paton and Ian Bairnson. (*Arista*)

Above: An EMI publicity shot inside the cockpit of a Concorde in early 1975. (*Alamy*)

Right: A publicity shot from 1974. (*Alamy*)

Right: Auditioning bass players for the debut Pilot tour. Abbey Road Studio 2. London 1974. *(David Paton Collection*)

Left: An early Pilot publicity shot from 1974. *(David Paton Collection*)

Right: On *TopPop* miming to 'January' in 1975.

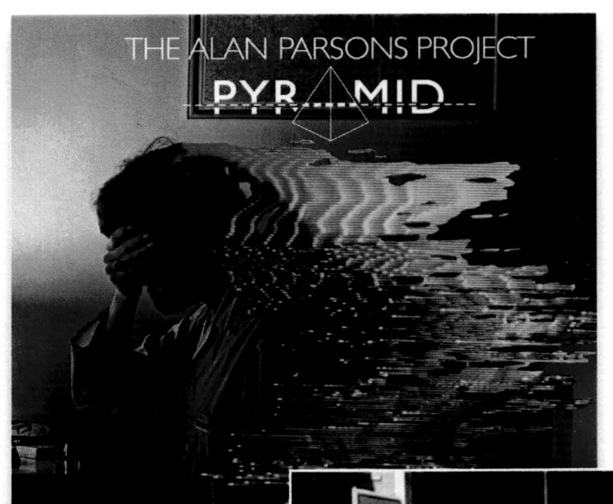

Left: The Alan Parsons Project album, *Pyramid*. Featuring 'What Goes Up', which I sang. (*Arista*)

Right: An early experiment in Abbey Road, recording via an android head in 1976. *(David Paton Collection*)

Left: A live performance with Rick Wakeman from *The Classical Connection* in 1991.

Above: The Elton John Band in South America in 1996. *(David Paton Collection*)

Left: With Elton John in Australia in 1986. *(David Paton Collection*)

Below: The Elton John Band: Davey Johnstone, Elton John, David Paton in the USA in 1986. *(David Paton Collection*)

Left: Meeting the inspirational Uncle Max in Australia during the Countdown Spectacular Tour in Sydney, 2007. (*David Paton Collection*)

Right: A still from a video recorded with my friend Kenny Herbert in 2008. *(David Paton Collection*)

Pilot at The Kings Theatre Edinburgh. (*Stuart Stott*)

Right: Dalkeith Country Park 2014. Myself, Ian Bairnson and Stuart Tosh. Our final Pilot concert together. *(David Paton Collection)*

Left: At the Jamhouse, Edinburgh, around 2011. (*Stuart Stott*)

Right: *A Pilot Project* CD cover in 2014.

Above: Having a play together at Ian and Leila's house in Scotland in 2018. (*Leila Bairnson*)

Left: A return to Wuppertal. A break during rehearsals in 2018. (*Dave Stewart*)

Left: At home in Buckstone Road, Edinburgh, in 1977 with my daughter Sarah. *(David Paton Collection*)

Above: The Grandkids. Jackson, Ava and Baby Jamie. *(David Paton Collection*)

Left: Granddaughter Ava McPhail. *(David Paton Collection*)

Above: Grandkids Ava and Jackson having fun in my studio. *(David Paton Collection)*

Below: With my daughters Katy and Sarah in Dalkeith in 2014. *(David Paton Collection)*

Above: Mary and friend in Australia in 1987. *(David Paton Collection)*

Right: Mary and I on Hogmanay at Archerfield, North Berwick, in 2016. *(David Paton Collection)*

Above: Mary and I in the control room of Studio Three, Abbey Road. February 18, 2023. (*Mary Paton*)

Above: Having makeup applied for the Ozempic video shoot at Abbey Road. (*Mary Paton*)

Left: Lights, camera, action. Recording some guitar licks for the Ozempic version of 'Magic'. Thankfully the cameras weren't too distracting. (*Mary Paton*)

were being used for empire-building and I knew I could bring it to an end if I didn't overreact and planned well. I was determined to put a stop to it. We were responsible for the success, and I don't think it was greed that motivated me to put an end to them having control of our earnings.

I put it to the management that I needed to move house as the one-bedroom tenement flat was inadequate. They reluctantly agreed to put up some money as long as I took out a 50% home loan. There was no holding me back now. Being aware of London house prices, I started to check out the houses in The Braids, Edinburgh. Mary and I found a house that we liked on Braid Road, and we managed to secure it. Things were getting better, but I wasn't going to stop there.

Thick made the mistake of leaving me alone in the Knightsbridge office for ten minutes while he attended to some other business. Within that time, I'd noticed a royalty statement on his desk made out to David Paton c/o Pilot management. It was for a substantial amount and had already been paid into their account. I kept it quiet but started making inquiries about my earnings from record sales, publishing and PRS performing rights. It was also time to meet with EMI to ask for advice and help with our management problems.

Billy announced that he wanted to leave the band and pursue a solo career. I tried to talk him out of it, but he was being egged on by his boyfriend, and the management probably saw it as an opportunity to obtain another recording advance. There was no animosity between Billy and me. I was just disappointed that he wanted to split up the partnership that had been so successful. But he was being promised a lot. Our manager's wife took him under her wing; they went shopping together as she helped groom him for his shot at stardom. Using his full Christian name of William also appealed to Billy. The management negotiated his solo deal with EMI records and despite the split, we all contributed to Billy's album *Solo Casting*. He even managed to get Phil Collins in on drums. But without Billy, Pilot would never be the same. I started writing for the next album and the songs began to reflect how I was feeling with titles like 'Lies and Lies', 'Too Many Hopes', 'Penny in My Pocket' and 'First After Me'. The optimism and sense of hope were leaving my writing and it was being replaced by disappointment, frustration and lack of interest.

But that selfish thought of pursuing a solo career never entered my head. I enjoyed being in a band. It was really the end of the dreams we'd shared as musicians and Billy was blinded by his own ego. It's an age-old story now that when a band member decides to go solo, some have success and some have failure. Billy was encouraged to get out of Pilot and be a solo artist. I told him what I thought, but I knew that it was looked upon as sour grapes. Billy had a boyfriend encouraging him, management encouraging him and a whole entourage of sycophantic friends pushing him forward and telling him he was better than Pilot. So, in the end, I found it quite sad to watch the inevitable unfold. I've learned a lot about people and what success can do to them. Their desire for fame is very selfish, destructive and pathetic. Billy began his career as a very humble guy, but I saw such a change in him. It was very sad to watch that ego develop and overtake his logic and sensibility. I didn't really recognise him in the end.

Canada and the third album

Meanwhile, Pilot carried on with only three wheels on the wagon. I had no real enthusiasm for the band, although I wasn't ready to jump ship, despite the problems. We decided it was time to beef up the sound, so we started looking for another producer for the next album. We met with Gus Dudgeon, who has produced Elton, Bowie, Chris Rea, The Zombies and way too many artists to list here. He went on to become a great friend and was responsible for me working with Elton, although, sadly, Gus and his wife Sheila were killed in a car crash on the M4 in 2002.

We met with Gus at the EMI offices in Manchester Square. After chatting for a while and hearing how unhappy we were with our management, he said, 'You guys seem to have a lot of internal problems and you need to sort them out before I'll work with you'. With that, he left the meeting. I respected Gus and he shot from the hip. Of course, he was right. We had a lot of trouble in the camp and Gus picked up on it very quickly. Roy Thomas Baker, who produced Queen, was brought in. He was quite a flamboyant, adventurous type and under his guidance, we agreed to record the next album in Super Bear, Morin Heights, Quebec, Canada.

Super Bear was a famous studio. The Bee Gees, David Bowie, Rush and Cat Stevens had all recorded there. Stuart brought his new girlfriend, Ellyn, out after a couple of days and while that was OK at the time, she was always there, like Stuart's shadow. It became a little irritating for me, as we needed to work and Ellyn was a bit of a distraction for Stuart, but with the benefit of hindsight, it probably wasn't that bad. Perhaps I felt like I was competing for his attention, asking him to help me out with some backing vocals or in adding some percussion. But Stuart never let me down, his playing and singing were faultless, and I was probably behaving like a spoiled brat.

I arranged for Mary to join me in Canada after a few days; we just needed time to get all the hard work out the way before she arrived. When Mary came, she complained of feeling unwell, so we called the doctor. He diagnosed flu and she was ordered to stay in bed for ten days. She was well taken care of by Roy's wife, Barbara while I was in the studio. But I was really worried about her.

When Mary started to recover, I could see that she'd lost a lot of weight, but she bounced back quickly and was soon enjoying all the fun of being in Canada. My Super 8 movie camera helped preserve some of the fun we experienced back then.

As we continued with the album, all of the backing tracks had been recorded, but Roy felt that we should add another up-tempo song. We all liked the Craighall demo of Billy's song 'Maniac', but I felt it needed a chorus, so I wrote that in the studio on the piano with Billy in mind while everyone was waiting to do a take on the song.

I never believed the life that you lead,
I never could doubt that luck would run out,
Open your eyes you never did realise,
Open your mind but look out from behind.

Yes, there's a little bit of venom in that lyric. I was hurt that Billy was leaving us. He was the one guy I felt was on the same level as me in terms of songwriting. The two of us started it all, there was strength in the partnership, and I didn't want to lose it. The essence of Pilot was Billy and I and for me, no-one else could take his place. We were the creative ones and without the partnership, there was nothing. Meanwhile, Billy was writing 'Truly Fruity Flavour Has Us All' as a little dig at me and my so-called simple songs.

Canada was a winter wonderland. The houses looked like picture postcards with the snow on the rooftops and the orange glow of the lanterns on the porches. A thick layer of snow covered everything; the roads were cleared by snowploughs but still remained covered with hard-packed snow.

We had two hire cars and looked forward to the drive back from the studio in the evening to our large cabin which was on three floors. As we approached the turn-off to the cabin, Roy would pull on the hand brake and put the car into a broadside so that we slid around the corner.

We sometimes made it around, but on other occasions, we ended up ploughing into the snow drifts and up the ten-foot walls of snow banking, howling with laughter. Boys will be boys.

Every morning before studio work, we went skiing together. It was marvellous; what a great way to start the day. At the dinner table one evening, Mary recalled the events of the day while skiing with Barbara, who is German. The T-bar is used to pull you up to the top of the slopes; it fits between your legs and you kind of sit on it. While using the T-bar the guys helping the skiers were patting Mary's bum as they pretended to help her. The third time it happened, she told Barbara what they were doing. Apparently, Barbara made them all lineup and asked them, 'which one of you is touching her bottom'. We all laughed out loud when she told us that, but understandably she wasn't happy with their behaviour. Barbara joined in from the other side of the table with, 'it's ridiculous – I think they should all be shot'.

Stuart and I worked in the studio together, laying down backing vocals. It was a lot of work for us as Roy liked to layer everything three or four times. Stuart recalls: 'I remember the complexity of the backing vocals on 'Maniac'. Roy had us singing parts of a word and every other word of a sentence in order to get the stereo separation'.

I don't think I've ever done a similar vocal track since!

We had almost finished the backing vocals when we had an emergency. Ellyn had broken her leg while skiing. Ellyn was a very wealthy girl, and she lived in New York. She was initially seen by a doctor in Canada but insisted on flying to New York to see her own specialist. Ellyn and Stuart invited Mary to join them, and I told her it would be good for her to see New York, so she was happy to go while I carried on with Roy finishing the vocal overdubs, which were laborious and time-consuming.

The band and crew wanted to go into town for a drink and a game of pool. I said I had work to do, so I stayed behind. I had the place to myself and needed to finish off the lyrics for a song we had recorded called 'Too Many Hopes'. It was a beautiful evening and I sat upstairs with a guitar and a roaring wood-burning fire. I had a glass of wine and a gorgeous starry sky and the frozen lake glistening under the full moon, visible through the large panoramic window. There, I wrote these words ...

Cold so deep and eyes that weep,
alone from the rest of the crowd.
Too many hopes when I'm down,

too many hopes.
Dream away a lazy day,
alone with my head in a cloud,
too many hopes when I'm down,
too many hopes.

I felt alone but happy.

The following day Mary, Stuart and Ellyn returned from New York buzzing. Ellyn was on the mend, and they had had a great trip. As the backing vocals were now complete, Stuart set off to Montreal with Ellyn for a couple of days. That was the kind of life we had then. It was a real privilege to live and work like that.

The end of Pilot mark one

On returning from Canada, I set up a meeting with EMI to discuss the management problems. Stuart, Ian and I arrived to find a new head of A&R, Bob Mercer. We were invited to his office and were surprised when he introduced his lawyer to us and began by telling us that all questions we had would be answered by said lawyer. That was not very friendly or helpful, and we were dismayed. We needed help and if EMI had fully understood what we were up against, I'm sure they might have offered an olive branch at least. The lawyer produced a list of the advances paid by EMI to the management and we were shocked.

I wanted out, away from the management who, from my point of view, had destroyed what should have been the happiest time of our lives. I wrote to the EMI royalties department and to PRS, informing them that I wanted all royalties paid directly into my bank account from now on. I'm not money motivated and my actions did help save me from financial ruin, but they didn't stop the rot; that was out of my control. Whatever it was that Billy and I were working towards in the Craighall days had now evolved into a nightmare.

Stuart and I had a silly fall out about Ellyn being everywhere; she was at photo shoots fixing his hair, at interviews, at recordings, and the final straw came when we were doing a Saturday morning TV show and the presenter Sally James asked for Stuart and me to make our way onto the set. Ellyn stood up with Stuart and with anger I said to her, 'Where the fuck are you going'. That was it for Stuart, I'd insulted his girl and he'd pissed me off by not keeping her away when we had work to do, so he decided he'd had enough from me and he quit the band. I'm happy to say that he went on to join 10cc. Stuart would never be short of work as he is an excellent drummer and remains a lifelong pal despite our falling out back then. He also joined Billy, Ian and me for the first two Alan Parsons Project albums.

I seem to have reached a negative part of my recollections and I wish I could inject some hope or humour into it, but I wouldn't be telling the whole story if I just glossed over the facts as I remember them. I don't want it to sound like I'm a victim, either. I'm not; it's all part of the apprenticeship of being in the music business – what you might call a learning curve. We made the initial mistake of engaging Thick and Dim as our managers and we were paying for that mistake as we didn't cross the T's and dot the I's when we should have,

I'm certainly no angel and if the Pilot story had been written by another band member, you might have heard a variation on these events. What I remember are the things that affected me personally, the events that left their mark and that's why I still remember them to this day. The words of Charles Dickens seem to sum it up perfectly for me:

> It was the best of times; it was the worst of times. It was the age of wisdom,
> it was the age of foolishness.

It is a pity that such a great opportunity was ruined by greed, stupidity, ego and thoughtlessness. I know of many musicians who had a lot more success than me, but they couldn't handle it – not just financially but mentally, physically, and emotionally. So in that respect, I count my blessings. I may have a few regrets, but I realise that events were out of my hands.

It was now time to collect my thoughts and decide what to do next.

Back home in Edinburgh, I was relaxed. I was resting, recovering, and planning. Dim called to say I was needed for another TV show, but I told him I wouldn't be doing anything else for Pilot. He threatened me by saying, 'if you don't do this TV show, you'll never work in the music industry again'. I believed him. My back was against the wall, and I had no option but to do the show. I've watched that performance on YouTube and I certainly don't look like I'm happy to be there. It was ironic to be appearing on that *Arrows* TV show singing 'Penny In My Pocket', a song about not having the money for a tube train or taxi to the studio. It was written as I walked from my hotel to Abbey Road a few years previously.

After the TV show, I was able to return home to my safe haven and I really thought that would be the end of the Pilot chapter. As a final insult, Dim sent me a chain letter and he wrote along the top, 'Send this on to ten people; it might give you some luck, and let's face it, you need some luck'. I ripped it up and put it in the bin.

Predictably, my salary stopped and so did my mortgage payments. Royalties are paid every three months and as I hadn't received any royalty payments at that time, there was no income at all. The stress was enormous. Mary and I were having a really hard time of things, and our relationship was suffering. I had to sell the house on Braid Road. We found a buyer pretty quickly and started the search for a home that we could afford to buy on a limited income. We found a newly built home on the Buckstone housing estate, which lies to the south of the Braid Hills. But a week before the move, I received my first royalty cheque, which was the beginning of a new and happily secure future for us. I must say that we had a few good years on the Buckstone estate and made many new friends. Furthermore, being away from the management was like a cloud lifting and I could see things a lot more clearly.

I only had one more year under contract to them and whatever I got involved in now would certainly be with me taking a back seat and low-profile, with no pressure and no limelight. The management had no control over me as an individual, only as a member of Pilot. Many media people wanted interviews, but I refused to talk and was glad I'd stayed in Edinburgh. It was a great relief to forget about being a musician for a while and devote my time to Mary and Sarah. We were now settled after a terrible period of uncertainty, insecurity and many tears of unhappiness, but it made us stronger and together, we eventually embraced a time of real happiness. I thought I could sit it out until the contract expired and then decide what I wanted to do next.

But it wasn't going to end there.

The Alan Parsons Project and a Pilot Revival

I didn't have to wait long or look very far for the wheels to start rolling again. Eric Woolfson called me and started to explain his ideas for a concept album based on the work of Edgar Allan Poe. He told me that Alan Parsons would be producing the album.

Eric was born into a Jewish family in the Charing Cross area of Glasgow, where his family owned the Elders furniture store. He moved to London in 1963 and established himself as a songwriter, lyricist, vocalist, executive producer and session pianist. I'd seen Eric with Alan a few times in the canteen at Abbey Road and found out he would be involved with Alan as his manager. But I had no idea they were going to be creating a long-lived musical partnership as well.

Eric's phone call came at the right time for me, and I was eager to get involved with his project. It seemed like the perfect next step for me and exactly what I wanted. It was low profile; there would be good music and no pressure. Eric had also asked Billy, Stuart and Ian to play on the first album *Tales of Mystery and Imagination*, so this would be Pilot back together again in Studio Two, Abbey Road, with Alan Parsons producing. The icing on the cake would be that there would be no 'evil eye' management.

Over the years, we became well-known faces at Abbey Road. We even had the privilege of parking in the car park out front and we were on first-name terms with the studio manager and his employees. But on this first occasion the studio was empty when we arrived and offloaded our gear. Billy and Stuart arrived and we made our way down to the canteen. We were greeted by Eric and Alan and joined them for coffee. There was an air of excitement as Eric explained a little more about his ideas for the future and told us he wanted a long-term commitment to what he knew would be a very successful project. He also made it clear that he wanted Pilot to add their own magic to help enhance his music. His enthusiasm rubbed off on us all and we were all keen to get in the studio and start shaping the songs.

The recordings got off to a great start and I was very impressed with Eric's songwriting and piano playing. He had a happy way of putting over his music to us and it did feel like a band – a really good studio band. It was a while since Pilot had played together as a unit, but we still had that quality that helped give The Project the sound of a really tight-knit group of musicians.

We spent a lot of time reshaping the songs and working on suitable instrumental sections. Many suggestions from the band were implemented to enhance the overall arrangements. That goes well beyond the job of being a session musician, which is what Alan Parsons has continued to describe us as over the years. I would also add acoustic guitar, backing vocals and the occasional lead vocal, as well as playing bass. We had a great working relationship and most of the time, the music went really well.

I remember recording the thunderclap for *Tales of Mystery and Imagination*. It was a Sunday afternoon and we thought it would be a good idea to set a microphone up outside the back door of Studio Two. Eric, Stuart and I agreed to stand outside under umbrellas and place an android head on a stand with a microphone built into each of its ears. This was supposed to pick up the sound exactly as a human would hear it, as we were in the middle of one of the best thunder and lightning storms that London had seen or heard in a long time. Alan was up in the control room with the tape running in record and waiting for the ideal thunderclap. It came and was so spectacular that Eric and I looked at each other and he burst out laughing. Of course, I couldn't control myself. It was just that look in his eyes and the expression on his face; we were like a couple of kids at a firework display. Needless to say, we ruined the recording. Alan was none too chuffed and stormed down the stairs very angrily – a rare sight. But we did capture another clap just a few minutes later and all was forgiven. Eric and I always had wry smiles on our faces whenever we listened to the playback of that moment.

Another time after we'd been for dinner to Eric's favourite restaurant Keats, Billy was asked to play flute. He had already played a good part, but Eric wanted him to play something different. He left the control room and walked downstairs to speak to Billy. Eric was not happy; he was trying to explain what he heard in his head and Billy was getting frustrated with him. They started to have a heated discussion and we watched as Eric pulled the flute from Billy's hands and bent it between his hands and his knee. Whether it was intentional to damage the flute or not, I don't know. But that was too much for Billy and he left the studio, never to return to work with Eric or the Project ever again. I believe Eric paid for the flute to be repaired. Apart from that little hiccup, it was generally a lot of fun and we all worked hard together as a team – with the music being uppermost on our priority list.

When Eric wrote 'Eye in the Sky', I remember Alan saying it would never be a hit song. Eric was adamant that it would be released as a single and it would top the charts. They even had a wager on whether or not it would be a hit. Eric won that bet, hands down. In August 1982, 'Eye in the

Sky' reached number three on the *Billboard* charts in the USA. In October 1982, it reached number one in both Canada and Spain.

There was a standard routine for recording the Project albums. The sessions were open-ended, so there was no stop time. We just finished when we became tired or when we'd completed the work we had scheduled for the day. The studio was booked 24 hours a day for a period of roughly six to eight weeks. Getting the basic tracks down would generally take about two weeks, but sometimes it could take from noon till two or three in the morning to get a piece of music sounding the way we wanted it to sound. Eric would play his songs a few times on the piano. We would all take notes and then have a play-through together. I enjoyed finding the right bass part for the song; it's very satisfying to know that the part I'm playing is gelling with all the other instruments, but we were all given the freedom to play what we felt worked for the song. The more we played the piece, the tighter the drums and bass became. I'd be listening to the bass drum, in particular. Sometimes Stuart would ask what I was playing so that we could work the drums around my part or vice versa. We'd try a take, then go up to the control room for a listen; there might be suggestions for another approach, change the drum pattern, maybe a different tempo, different key maybe, faster, slower or more commas. Sometimes the song would develop into something that was completely unrecognisable from its original concept. So, it was a day of playing the song over and over again until it was right and everybody was happy. That was fine; we were all focused on getting it perfect and time always flew by. Our twelve-hour day could pass in what seemed like no time at all.

So, about 10 to 14 days would see the end of the basic tracks being recorded. For me, there would be another couple of weeks of overdubbing acoustic guitars and vocal harmonies. At the overdub stage, some of my studio time could be spent watching and waiting while someone else added an embellishment. So it was essential to have some form of entertainment to help pass the time. We tended to call each other by our surnames for some reason; I think it was Eric that started that. We played a lot of pool. Eric was a demon at it. He'd say, 'fancy a game, Paton? I'll play you for a fiver. If I won, he'd say, 'right, double or quits'. This would go on until he won completely, or we had to break and do some work. 'Blow it out your arse, Woolfson' became a common saying. It came about when Eric was boasting about his skills on the pool table. I think it was Stuart Elliott who first said it, and it became a well-used phrase after that and always had us laughing, especially if it was shouted out by one of us when the red light went on and we were about to do a take.

Ian and I set up the model car racing game Scalextric in the corner of the studio and Paul and Linda McCartney once joined us for a race. We never got bored – it was such a pleasure to be there, and the novelty never wore off. When I was actively involved in the overdubbing process, it was all-consuming. I could spend hours in the control room watching Alan at the mixing desk doing his work and listening to the music developing into the distinctive sound of The Alan Parsons Project. I learned a lot from doing just that.

Eric would usually sing along as we ran through the song in the studio. When we started recording tracks, there was no vocal as Eric would be concentrating on his keyboard playing. When we finally got the take we were happy with, Eric would usually record a guide vocal. That guide vocal would be used as a template for any guest vocalists. So, if I was doing a lead vocal, I'd have a fair idea of the melody before it came to recording my voice. I'd spend a while in the studio with just Eric and Alan and it could take a few hours to complete all the voices as Alan was very particular about the double tracking being perfectly in sync with the original voice (double tracking is the act of recording a vocal part two times at least, attempting to match the vocal performance as closely as possible to the first). The harmonies were given the same amount of attention and every voice was double-tracked. That was a big part of the Project sound and identity, almost as much as the bass playing and the guitar work of Ian Bairnson. When Ian and I recorded the acoustic guitar parts, we would play together and then double-track the guitars. A lot of the guitar solos had the same treatment.

We followed the same format for all the albums. I played on nine of the ten Project albums, with *Gaudi* the only one I was unavailable for.

We didn't always record in Abbey Road. In 1978 we travelled to France to record *Eve* at Super Bear Studios in Nice. We travelled to Paris in 1979 to record *The Turn of a Friendly Card* at Acousti studios. *Stereotomy* was recorded in1984 at Mayfair studios, London. The spark did start to fade towards the end, and the songs were not being written as prolifically or enthusiastically as they originally were. There was some kind of friction between Clive Davis of Arista Records and Eric Woolfson. So much so that *The Sicilian Defence* album was little more than a contractual obligation album with a lot of ideas coming together in the studio. In fact, for one song, Eric sat at the piano, played the note C and said to us all, 'so guys, what can you do with that?'

I tried hard to convince everyone that it would be a great idea to take the Project on the road. My voice fell on deaf ears. Alan and Eric didn't have much enthusiasm for live work at that time and the band wouldn't make a move in that direction as they thought Alan and Eric would object. I knew it was possible and was very frustrated with all of them. It wasn't until record sales tailed off that Alan approached us to perform a one-off gig in Antwerp in 1990 as the original line-up. That was the only gig that I performed with The Alan Parsons Project. At last, we were playing live together and it sounded great. We were joined by Gary Brooker of Procol Harum fame, who had featured on the Project album *Stereotomy*, singing 'Limelight', another classic Eric Woolfson song. Rehearsals went very smoothly and the atmosphere was full of joy and optimism. It could – and should – have happened fifteen years earlier when the Project was going strong.

The Project albums sold over 50 million copies worldwide. There is no obligation for any artist to present musicians with gold discs for their contribution to the work – it's a courtesy. But none of the band received gold discs for their work with the Project. It's a great shame, as all it takes is a phone call to the record company and many artists do reward musicians with gold discs, Elton John being a prime example. But Eric and Alan didn't want the band to receive any publicity at all. All we were given were credits on the album sleeves for our substantial contributions.

The main contributor behind the Project was Eric Woolfson. It was his concept and his music. It was around 2007 that he began to organise a tour and he called us all and started to get the ball rolling. But sadly, Eric passed away on December 2 2009 before his plans came to fruition, dashing any hope of that band's original members playing Project music together again. Eric wrote the majority of the songs, while Alan wrote a few instrumentals. But all the songs are listed as Woolfson/Parsons compositions and I presume Eric did that to help get Alan on board with his Project ideas. It was also Eric who gave The Alan Parsons Project its name. I mention this because I believe that Eric has not been given the full recognition that he deserves for the success of the Project.

Alan was very much the producer. He was a very fine one, although his talents as a musician were pretty basic. But he continues to tour with his American band, which sadly contains no original band members in The Alan Parsons Live Project.

1977. The Pilot Revival. Two's a Crowd.

The Alan Parsons Project was signed to Arista records with the main man at the label being Clive Davis. Eric Woolfson was on friendly terms with Thick and Dim and together, they hatched a plan for Ian Bairnson and me to sign with Arista as Pilot. They wanted us to record an album with Alan Parsons producing. I wasn't keen to be involved with Thick and Dim again, but with reassurance from Eric (who I trusted and respected), I agreed to the recording of another album – so long as the brothers stayed away from us and the studio. My contract with them was soon to expire and another Pilot album could be a great vehicle for the songs I was still writing.

Ian did not have a personal contract with the management and agreed to sign with them for five years. He also signed a publishing contract with them. But I told them I would never sign any contract with them again.

We flew to New York to meet with Clive Davis and sign the contract. It was my first trip there and I was excited about it. The boy in me took over and images from my DC and Marvel comics started to appear in my mind. I half-expected to see Superman swoop along 5th Avenue on his way to a crime scene. America had always fascinated me from as far back as I can remember. I remember when I was at primary school, I drooled at my friend Dougie McCandlish wearing his cowboy shirts sent from relatives in the USA. New York fascinated me. So did the cars and the skyscrapers. It was the land of Highway Patrol, Roy Rogers and Laurel and Hardy. I was here! We stayed only a few days and Clive was the perfect host. He entertained us in the evenings – it was nothing too fancy, but it was a good taste of the real New York. He even took us clubbing; we felt privileged to be in such VIP company.

We were supposed to receive our share of the advance but guess what? Thick and Dim didn't want to part with it. The brothers kept coming up with excuses for not paying us our share. Ian and I contacted Mickey Shapiro. He was the USA lawyer who negotiated the deal with Arista. He told Ian and me that the money had already been paid to the brothers. He said they would be coming to his hotel to meet him the next evening and that we should be there when they arrived. The brothers had no idea Ian and I would be there, so when they arrived, Mickey really brought them down a peg and insisted that they take Ian and I to their office and pay us the sum we were due. So we drove to their office and when we arrived, Thick said they could only give us part of the money due and made up some petty excuse for not having the full amount that was owed to us. We took the cheques they wrote out for us and never received a penny more.

Clive made it clear that he wanted me to write another song like 'Magic' or 'January', so I set to work on a song that would express my feelings about self-motivation. As soon as we returned back to the UK, I got down to writing. 'Get Up and Go' started to take shape. In the verse, I sing about using excuses not to work: 'Oh, but the room it was icy cold; maybe tomorrow night' – but the chorus is full of optimism. If you're going to achieve something, it's all down to you and nobody else will do it for you. Clive loved the song and sent a telegram saying it was going to be a smash hit. If only it had been. It wasn't. But it did well enough to keep the Pilot name alive worldwide. When I think back on the song titles on that album, I realise I was 'telling it like it is'. I was revealing my thoughts, saying what I should have been saying to the people I'd been surrounded with. 'Library Door' was the song I wrote for Billy at the start of our dream. 'Evil Eye' was written for Thick and Dim, and they knew I'd written it for them. 'Mr Do Or Die' was another one written for Billy. I thought he was out of control at that time and, well, one of the advantages of being a songwriter is being able to say something in a song that you wouldn't normally say to a person directly.

> All around from the highest ground I was lost in a dream of a kind,
> Evil eye you were standing by with trouble for my mind.

I was informed that the follow-up single to 'Get Up and Go' would be 'Running Water'. It's a good song, although a bit of a dirge. It was written by Ian, but it sounds nothing like a catchy Pilot hit. It was possibly no coincidence that because Ian wrote the song, Thick and Dim owned the publishing meaning that is was more likely to be chosen as a single. 'Running Water' bombed and the Arista contract ended after a year.

I feel bad that a lot of the loyal fans wanted to hear more from Pilot. It really was impossible to carry on under these conditions. We'd been ripped off and torn apart, and it soured what should have been the best time of our lives. That's life – you live and learn. When one chapter comes to an end, you should move on and not keep trying to resurrect something that has already run its course.

Meanwhile, I was doing well with my session work and I just counted my blessings that I could make a good living from music despite the setbacks. So, after the limited release of the album *Two's a Crowd*, Pilot took time out with no thoughts of further activity. It took a very long time for us to find our wings again.

Paul McCartney

I consider myself extremely lucky to be a musician and to have achieved a degree of success, and because of that, I've been able to be in the company of other musicians of whom I'm totally in awe.

I first met Paul McCartney while we were recording *I Robot* with the Alan Parsons Project in Studio Two at Abbey Road. Alan told me that Paul would be coming by around midnight to finish mixing a track that Alan was engineering.

I was so excited at the prospect of meeting him. Alan was mixing and I was leaning over the mixing desk when Paul and Linda arrived. The playback was loud, but we made eye contact and smiled. Honestly, I couldn't believe I was in the same room as Paul and could hardly contain myself. After a few minutes, Paul made his way over towards me and he asked me if I had a cigarette, I said no, but I asked Alan if he had one, which Alan didn't hear as the music was too loud. Paul was telling me not to worry, but it was too late, Alan motioned to the tape operator to stop the tape. But oh no, I didn't want that to happen. It was so embarrassing, there was a difficult silence and I said again to Alan 'do you have a cigarette for Paul'. I still cringe to this day when I recall that episode. We left and let Alan get on with the work he was doing for Paul.

Shortly after that, we were working in Studio Three when Paul walked in with his engineer Geoff Emerick, who had also been The Beatles' engineer. Paul said to us, 'I'd love to have some Scottish voices on my latest recording. Can you pop along to Studio Two and sing for me? I'll give you a wee dram'. Ian and I were thrilled and Alan joined us. We all gathered in the control room and Geoff played us the song – it was 'Mull of Kintyre'. Of course, we loved it and made our way downstairs to the studio. We all stood in a circle around the microphone and the playback started. I was so delighted to be standing beside my idol, singing his song.

After the session, Paul and Linda said to me, 'come along anytime you want to'. Well, I didn't make a pest of myself, but I did go along a couple of times while Ian was doing overdubs. The first time I looked in, the door was open and Linda was sitting on her own. She asked me in and beckoned me to sit beside her. We chatted about what we were working on and she really made me feel at ease. We then got on to talking about Scotland and she reached down and opened a photograph album. Linda was showing me photos of the farm in Kintyre. She was flicking through the pages when Paul arrived with a few others. I took that as my cue to leave, embarrassingly banging my head against the side of the sloping ceiling as I was saying goodbye. I get so nervous meeting icons and become really awkward.

The second time I went along, I knocked on the door and slowly entered to see Paul sitting on his own, smoking a joint. He was facing the door with a small table and chairs in front of him. He said, 'come in, sit down'. The joint was pretty small, but he offered it to me and I accepted it. There was a guitar lying in an open case on the floor and I could see that it was left-handed. I asked him about 'Blackbird' and he picked up the guitar and played a little for me. I was delighted – blown away, in fact. The joint had gone out by this time, so I put it in the ashtray. Paul picked it up and relit it, took a couple of puffs and handed it back to me. We smoked it till it was tiny and difficult to hold. Sharing a joint with Paul was a big honour – a bit like passing the peace pipe. It was a real connection. We met a few times and, as mentioned, he even played Scalextric with Ian and me on the floor of Studio Two.

At one time, a bit later, when Abbey Road was having an anniversary event, I invited Mary along as I knew there would be many famous faces there. We met Sting, and Paul was there with Linda. He approached Mary and me and said hello. I introduced Mary. He started singing an old Scottish song, 'Bonnie Mary of Argyle,' in a very convincing Scottish accent.

I also remember my friend Bobby Heatlie being there. He's a songwriter from Edinburgh and he wrote 'Merry Christmas Everyone' for 1980s icon Shakin' Stevens. He had a Scottish singer with him, her name was Aneka, who had a hit with a song Bobby had written called 'Japanese Boy'. I said hello to Bobby, and he introduced Aneka. She blanked us dismissively while scanning the room full of famous faces. I remember thinking it was a bit rude of her. Mary and I chatted to Bobby for a while, then moved on to talk to other people when Aneka came back to me and said, 'Sorry, I didn't know who you were. Bobby just told me you're the bass player with The Alan Parsons Project'.

Sometimes you have to be somebody before some people will talk to you.

I was asked by the producer Jon Kelly to record an album with an EMI artist. His name was John Townley, a very fine singer-songwriter. We were lucky enough to record his album *More Than A Dream* in Montserrat. When John tried to book George Martin's Air Studios in London, he was told that the studio was fully booked. John had been employed as an engineer at Air Studios and he told George Martin that he couldn't get booked in for the recording. George told him that the studio in Montserrat was free on the dates of the planned recording, and because John was a former employee and good friend, he offered the studio at a very competitive rate. EMI agreed to the budget and we booked the studio for three weeks. On keyboards, we had Max Middleton, on guitar Alan Murphy and on drums, Stuart Tosh. It was pretty exciting jetting off to Antigua and then catching a small plane to Montserrat.

The studio opened in 1979, and the technical specification was every bit as good as the London studio, although the location was somewhat superior. The first album recorded there was Climax Blues Band's 1979 *Reel to Reel* and the last album was the Rolling Stones' *Steal Wheels* in 1989. Indeed, many legendary artists recorded there, including The Police, Elton John, Stevie Wonder, Paul McCartney, Rush, Duran Duran, Black Sabbath and Dire Straits – to name just a few.

So we had three glorious weeks recording the tracks with John Townley and it really was a paradise. Between takes, we'd lie by the swimming pool and enjoy the breathtaking scenery. There was also a very fine golf course on Montserrat. Stuart Tosh is a very good golfer; he was a member of Wentworth golf club and lived very close to the clubhouse and so Stuart and I had a memorable game of golf surrounded by huge lizards that would get up on their hind legs and run off if you chased them.

We did meet Paul McCartney and the band as we drove down the dirt road from the studio to the beach, where we'd catch the small plane to Antigua. Paul and his band had just landed and were making their way up the single dirt road to the studio. We stopped as they approached, exchanged a quick chat and that was that. A few months later, I met up with Paul and Linda in Air studios in Oxford Circus and discussed Montserrat alongside various other topics.

On my 60th birthday, I was delighted to receive a framed birthday greeting and autograph from Paul, all thanks to my good friends John Glen and Kenny Herbert. John is a friend of Mark Hamilton, who is in charge of security for Paul and it was he who asked Paul to write a birthday greeting for me.

Sessions and Solo Recording

1977 and 1978. Kate Bush

Andrew Powell and I have been friends since he was brought into the Pilot camp as orchestral arranger. Andrew has many strings to his bow and is also a very fine producer, so he would call me with session work on a regular basis. To this day, we keep in touch and have written a few songs together for a future project.

He called me to say that he was producing an EMI artist named Kate Bush and would like me to play bass on her debut album. He explained that David Gilmour from Pink Floyd had received a tape of Kate's demos from his friend Ricky Hopper. He loved her voice and songwriting and wanted to help her if possible. So he travelled to meet Kate at her parents' house in Kent. She played David 40 or 50 songs from her demo tapes. He then played the tape to the EMI A&R department. I have read that the first song David Gilmore played was 'The Man With The Child In His Eyes'. That is when the ball started to roll, and according to Kate, this inspired her to write the song 'Them Heavy People', with it's opening lines 'rolling the ball'.

Andrew explained all of this to me and added that Kate was very young, very talented and very down-to-earth. The recordings took place in Air Studios, London, throughout July and August 1977. Ian Bairnson invited me to stay with him during the recording as I was still living in Edinburgh at that time. Ian lived in Bray in Berkshire, so it would take approximately 45 minutes to drive into central London. We arrived at the studio to be met by Andrew, Stuart Elliott (drums) and Duncan MacKay (keyboards). Andrew introduced us to Kate, and we set up and prepared to hear the music that she had written. We were all given chord charts from Andrew, which were very well-written and easy to follow. The charts consisted of chords with notation where necessary. It was a fantastic surprise for us when she sat at the piano and played through the first song. This girl was sensational. Her playing was flawless, her song was very well constructed and had immediate appeal, and her voice was very delicate and pitch-perfect. It was all relaxed and friendly and we were eager to play through the music.

When session musicians are presented with a chord chart, the producer/arranger is more or less saying play it as you feel it. When the music is well written (as Kate's music is), it's easy to be inspired by what you are hearing and, for me, constructing a bass part is a joy as it all comes together. It's also a big advantage to have all the musicians play together rather than just overdubbing individually. The music breathes much more when the musicians are constructing a part that is sympathetic to all the other players during the session. We all listen to each other and make the part we play work well with what the other musicians are doing. But when you are provided with notation, you must play the music as it's written. In most cases, with group sessions, it would just be the chord charts that we followed, so there was plenty of freedom. After the first run-through, Kate was absolutely delighted with what we were playing and she wanted us to play it through again. Each time we played it through, the arrangement got better and better until we were ready to do the first take. A first take is seldom the one we keep; it's more of a guideline for the musicians to listen to in the control room and have a better picture of how all the parts are working together. Mono headphones can be quite limiting, so it is much better to hear the song on the control room monitors.

We progressed through the recording of the songs at a steady pace and Kate was gelling with the players really well. It was a real pleasure to spend a few hours playing each song and perfecting our playing on each run-through. She adapted to her surroundings and quickly got into the way we went about constructing the elements of the songs.

With all the basic tracks completed, Ian and I did a few extra days for acoustic guitar and backing vocal overdubs. Ian then added the guitar solos. All in all, it had been a very positive and constructively enjoyable time making the album *The Kick Inside*. It was really great to watch Kate establish herself as a major artist and I am delighted to have been involved in her rise to success.

I didn't expect to be involved in any follow-up album, as is often the case with session musicians, but after the release and success of *The Kick Inside*, Andrew called to invite me to play on Kate's recording sessions for the follow-up, *Lionheart*. This time we'd be travelling to Super Bear Studios in Berre-les-Alpes on the French Riviera. Yes, we did enjoy the perks. Kate's live band, which included her boyfriend Del Palmer on bass, would also perform on a couple of the songs. I always found it a bit awkward meeting with her band, knowing that we were playing on the recordings and not them. They were fine musicians and all they were lacking was studio experience, but that experience is very important to the finished product. Del Palmer remains a friend and we have recollected those times very happily.

As we arrived at Super Bear, we were greeted by Kate and her band. It was a happy, friendly meeting and they told us how much we were going to enjoy the stay, as the cook was amazing and the grounds with a swimming pool were a delight. The band wished us a happy time and sped off in the minibus that we had arrived in. Oh yes, we did enjoy our time at Super Bear. The weather was perfect, the studio was a joy and the English chef was top-class.

Onto the music. The creative times with Kate in the studio continued. We had another really good selection of songs to play through and Kate was as happy as ever. She was even more relaxed with us now, and I really don't know how many times she asked me if I wanted a cup of tea. Of course, the studio had accommodation and we all had our own rooms, although we were together most of the day and in the evenings. Evening mealtimes were usually spent in conversation about the song arrangements and the plan for the following day. We did find time for swimming and lying in the sun, but we were there to work, and we did plenty of it. We were all sensible and responsible musicians and just got into a routine of breakfast, studio, lunch, studio and dinner, then studio until we were exhausted. We'd normally stop working before it got too late, but as there was no set time; it was open-ended. So, if everyone was still lively enough, we would just continue until our bodies told us to go to bed. This is a normal way to go about it, especially if it's a residential studio. Most evenings, we would continue after dinner, but sometimes, there would be technical issues to resolve that only involved Andrew and the engineers, or there might be a guitar or piano overdub. I suppose it could be described as a kind of shift work.

But when we finished the last song, we knew we'd be travelling home. That's not so easy when you're in such beautiful surroundings and making wonderful music. But all things must pass.

1979. Chris De Burgh

Andrew Powell called again, and asked if I was available for an album with Chris De Burgh. I enjoyed his early albums – especially *Spanish Train* and *At the End of a Perfect Day* albums – so it was a pleasure to be asked to play on the recording of his album *Crusader*. We recorded at Air Studios in Oxford circus, the same place we recorded The *Second Flight* album as Pilot and *The Kick Inside* with Kate Bush.

Chris was very good at performing his music, either with guitar or piano. It was like he was putting on a performance for us and he had our full attention. We were chatting between takes and I mentioned how much I enjoyed his music. The next day, he arrived at the studio with his previous albums and handed them to me. 'This is for you' he said – very kind and thoughtful of him.

Chris' band consisted of the usual suspects. Myself on bass, Stuart Elliott on drums, Ian on guitar and this time Mike Moran on keyboards. Andrew was producing and playing grand piano with Jon Kelly engineering.

Good songs and a good atmosphere are always welcome in a musician's working environment, and we had plenty of both of those on this session. Chris was always anxious to get on with the work, and I can still hear him going from room to room during the coffee break shouting, 'right, lads, back to work'.

We had a lovely meal in an Italian restaurant one evening. Chris and I were chatting when the restaurateur announced it was time for a singsong. He was handing out various percussion instruments and singing as he did so. Chris decided he was going to entertain the diners by singing to them. During a break in the singsong, with great confidence, Chris stood up and just started singing. He was in good form and the song was excellent. I'm not sure how many of the diners knew who he was, but they certainly enjoyed hearing him. He received a very enthusiastic applause.

In the end, the *Crusader* album turned out to be a lovely collection of songs.

I met Chris in Germany in 2018 when I was doing a TV show when I was playing with Albert Hammond. Chris was surrounded by security and no one could get near him. I suppose I was lucky to bump into him on his way to the stage, but he was friendly and happy to say hello.

1979. No ties, no strings

Back in London after recording the *Eve* album with The Alan Parsons Project, regular vocalist Chris Rainbow was having a playback of his solo album in Scorpio Sound studio. It was on the ground floor of Euston Tower, London. He invited me along. Chris had introduced me to his manager David Knights, who had been the bass player with Procol Harum and had a great inside knowledge of the music business. I liked David a lot; we got on well together and shared a lot of rock and roll experiences. He became my manager a few months before I attended Chris's playback.

The A&R department of EMI were among the guests and I watched as David mingled with them. He was talking to the head of the A&R department and they were both looking at me as they spoke. The playback began and we listened to the album. Chris was a very talented guy and the songs sounded really great; it was a stunning album. His vocal harmonies were always outstanding and played a big part in the arrangements of his songs. Indeed, you'd find it hard to believe that Chris had a really bad stammer when you listen to his outstanding vocal arrangements that were clearly heavily influenced by Brian Wilson's arrangements for The Beach Boys.

I left the studio with David and when we got out into the fresh air, he said to me (with a big smile on his face) I think you have a deal with EMI. He told me that the A & R guy had pointed to me and said, 'I want to sign him'. That really was all about being in the right place at the right time. This was unexpected, a complete surprise. I'd already been signed to EMI with Pilot, and now that the Pilot days were virtually over, the head of A&R wanted to sign me as a solo artist.

Within the week, David and I were in the offices of EMI discussing the future of David Paton, the solo artist. I was delighted that David was handling the legalities. Here was a man who was totally trustworthy; he just needed an artist to have some chart success, but I knew he was very capable of taking care of business. The signing went smoothly and this time, with David Knights as my manager, we did have the contract looked at by a lawyer who recommended a couple of alterations. After that was straightened out, I signed to EMI.

Abbey Road Studio Three was booked for the recording and I chose Tony Clarke to produce the songs. I stayed in a hotel in St. Johns Wood, which also meant that I would walk past Paul McCartney's house every day.

One evening, after finishing at the studio, I got back to the hotel and decided to have a drink at the bar. I'd been sitting there for 15 minutes or so when I saw the band Doctor Hook arrive. They checked in then their singer Dennis Locorriere came over to the bar. He sat next to me and ordered a drink. He looked at me and said, 'I know you, you're the guy from Pilot, I recognise you from the caricature on your album cover of *From the Album of the Same Name'*. We started to chat and I told him I was recording in Abbey Road. He wanted to come along the next day to see the studio. He then asked me if I liked a smoke, and I said yes, occasionally. So, Dennis, a crew member and I walked up to Dennis's room. We listened to some music and they proceeded to get me completely stoned with dope that blew my socks off. After an hour or so, I started to feel the room spinning and told the guys I'd had too much and needed to get back to my room. I walked along the corridor, banging off the walls and somehow found my room. The next morning, I didn't feel too good but managed to have some breakfast with no sign of Dennis. Then I made my way to the studio. The guys never arrived.

We were recording the first song for my solo album when Kate Bush appeared with Jon Kelly. They said that they'd like me to play bass on the next album. I wanted to do it, but they were starting in a few days' time and I had Studio Three booked for six weeks. I told them I'd ask EMI if we could rearrange the dates, so David Knights got on the case and tried to persuade EMI to change my studio time to a later date. But the powers that be at EMI said no, they couldn't move the dates as the studio was fully booked for the next year. I went along to Studio Two to tell Kate I couldn't change my studio booking. I did recommend John Giblin for the gig, and his bass playing on 'Babooshka' is top-class – he did a great job.

While working on the album in Studio Three as an EMI artist, I was invited to a celebration in Studio Two. It was something to do with an Abbey Road anniversary. There were a few well know faces there, including Andy Latimer of Camel, Paul McCartney and Sting. I was talking with Kate when she said that she wasn't comfortable being in the crowded studio and she asked me if there was somewhere we could go and have a smoke. I said that we could use Studio Three as I had it booked on an open-ended basis. I knew she didn't like crowds and I wanted to find somewhere private where she wouldn't be pestered, thinking she'd be able to relax in the studio. We'd been alone chatting for about 20 minutes when the studio door opened and there was Andy Latimer and a few others saying, 'we wondered where you'd gone to'. Well, that was the end of my quality time with Kate. Before long, there were about a dozen people in the control room and Kate had had enough. She left very surreptitiously. I did the same a few minutes after her.

When my album was completed, we had a playback for EMI in the studio. They offered a warm response, but there was no wild enthusiasm. The song that was chosen for the single was 'No Ties, No Strings'. Once again, this was a song that reflected my state of mind at this time. The album was on hold until EMI could see the reaction to the single, but the response was not encouraging, as we didn't pick up much airplay and so the album was withheld. After the first year, the option to continue the contract was not taken up by the label and the album was shelved.

On reflection, I realise I was ill-prepared for the recording of a solo album. I should have taken time out to write more songs – perhaps a cottage in the highlands of Scotland would have helped inspire me. I know that the songs I submitted for the album were not the best I could have delivered and if I'd sat down and written music with an album release in mind, I'd have had more songs to choose from. Instead, I picked songs that were already half-written with no end goal in mind apart from being for my amusement.

It's not a bad album, but it wasn't my best work.

1981. Chris Rea

Chris Rea is such a lovely guy, so down to earth and one of the boys. We first met outside Air Studios at a time when you could park on the street. His approach to the recordings was so relaxed and effortless. I found myself feeling totally at ease with Chris, just as I would with a mate. So for me, he *was* a mate. Recording and working with Chris was a breeze, as he was one of the band, so the whole process of working with him was a joy from start to finish. When we had a break, we'd sit in the control room and have casual conversations about everyday events. There was a lot of laughter and no pressure to hurry the work along. The session was for his fourth studio album, simply entitled *Chris Rea*, released in 1981. It charted on the UK album charts, peaking at number 52, while the single 'Loving You' peaked at number 65 on the UK singles chart, and charted on the US *Billboard* Hot 100 at 88. There were a lot of world-class musicians involved in the recordings of that album, including Max Middleton (keyboards), Pete Wingfield (keyboards), Jim Mullen (guitar), Ray Cooper (percussion) Katie Kissoon and Carol Kenyon on backing vocals and Dave Mattacks and Stuart Elliott on drums. There was also a young female assistant engineer by the name of Renate Blauel, who was to become Elton John's wife in 1984.

During the recordings, Chris was asked to do a live TV show and asked the band if we'd be willing to do the performance with him. It was a BBC TV afternoon show, so we only performed two songs. We were all happy to make ourselves available, as working with Chris was a joy. It was also refreshing to get out of the studio and into a live situation after some time. After the recording sessions were over, I didn't meet Chris again until 1997 at Elton's 50th birthday party at The Hammersmith Palais. Chris was wearing a Monks habit with exposed false boobs – very tasteful. When he asked me what I was up to, I told him I was ducking and diving, wheeling and dealing. So, very little at all, really!

1981. Elaine Paige

Elaine Paige had just had a top-five hit with 'Memory', a song from the musical Cats composed by Andrew Lloyd Webber, with lyrics by Trevor Nunn. The album I was involved in was simply entitled *Elaine Paige*, produced by Andrew Powell and Tim Rice and recorded at Air Studios, London.

It turned out that Elaine was a big Pilot fan, so we got on pretty well together. She asked me if I had any new songs, but quite honestly, I didn't have anything good enough, though she insisted that she wanted to hear what I had. I gave her a cassette of a few songs, but I don't remember any enthusiastic response from her. It didn't surprise me. Tim Rice was in the studio a lot of the time; he also spoke highly of the songs I had written for Pilot. I think that both Tim and Elaine expected me to present them with a song of the same calibre as 'Magic', but that was not going to happen. I'd taken my foot off the songwriting pedal and was writing mediocre songs at that time.

Elaine's album consisted of cover songs by many of my favourite writers. These included 'So Sad (To Watch Good Love Go Bad)' by Don Everly, 'Secrets' by Barry and Robin Gibb, 'Hot As Sun' by Paul McCartney and 'How The Heart Approaches What It Yearns' by Paul Simon. It was a pleasure to play these songs and she performed them very well. We also travelled to Monte Carlo to do a one-off show, which was great and she went down a storm. Afterwards, we all went to a club and drank champagne courtesy of the promoter. Elaine was on a high and was up dancing with various members of the band. Later, she invited us back to her hotel suite for drinks. All seemed to be going well until Elaine suddenly announced, 'right, I've had enough; everybody out'. OK, there was a lot of drink involved and she probably wanted to get some sleep. We all left quite hurriedly, although a little bemused at the abrupt end to the evening. But all was fine in the morning as we sat together for breakfast. Overall, I enjoyed working with Elaine and admire her voice and musicality.

1981. Jimmy Page . Death Wish 2 and 3.

Dave Mattacks called me and asked if I was available to do a session with Jimmy Page. I wanted to work with Jimmy – I love his playing and Led Zeppelin were a big influence on me. Dave said he didn't know much about the session except that it was for a soundtrack to a film, but I told him I'd love to do the session and he said he'd call back with more details.

Dave told me that Jimmy had been given a deadline of just a few weeks to write and record the album at his personal studio, The Sol, in Cookham in Berkshire. I was still living in Edinburgh at this time, so I decided to drive down with my basses and amp in the boot of the car.

The day before I was due to leave, I received a call from Jimmy Page. He said, 'you're supposed to be here today? we're all waiting for you'. He sounded a little angry, but I assured him that I was told by Dave that I wasn't due to start for another two days. He was a bit disgruntled but didn't lose his cool. I think he just accepted there had been a mix-up.

So I drove down from Edinburgh, arrived at The Sol studio and everything was very friendly. Jimmy was happy and enthusiastic about the project. He told me that movie director Michael Winner was his neighbour and that he had asked him to record a soundtrack for the film *Death Wish II*.

This was a new experience for me – performing along to a movie playback, with a time code and visuals to play to, so the timings had to be exactly right. Jimmy would play us his ideas then Dave and myself, along with Jimmy, would play together and get the music in shape. I really enjoyed the work and was given a completely free hand to do what I wanted. Jimmy was full of ideas and even had me running a coin slowly down the length of a bass string to record the sound. This really added to the tense atmosphere of both the visuals and the music. The whole session was like that; he was bursting with ideas and appeared delighted with my playing. The work was relaxed but focused and as soon as we had a good idea of the piece we were working on, we got our heads down and quickly got the track together.

It was so rewarding to watch Jimmy; he was always smiling and giving us thumbs up. Every time there was a drum fill or a bass lick, he'd become animated and looked so pleased with us.

After the session on day one, he invited us to a local Chinese restaurant for a meal. That was very enjoyable because we had a chance to just relax and chat. Also, the atmosphere was good because it was evident that Jimmy was delighted with the way things were developing in the studio. I know vocalist Chris Farlow was on the album, but I didn't have a chance to meet him as our work was over before the vocals were done.

In addition to the standard soundtrack release, a vinyl LP was released in Japan that featured rare outtakes from the Sol sessions. *Death Wish II* was released in CD format in 1999, but all CD versions of the album are now out of print. Used copies are highly collectable and can sell for over a hundred dollars.

The album was re-released by Jimmy Page exclusively through *www.jimmypage.com* on 1 December 2011 in a vinyl package that includes previously unreleased material and all-new 2011 sleeve notes and updated artwork. Only 1000 copies were released, with numbers 1–109 signed by Jimmy,

Jimmy said this to Chris Cornell in 2015. He seemed to enjoy my bass playing.

> I had a chance to go in the studio and do some really experimental stuff. Well, it was experimental to me. It involved a guitar synthesizer, and I was able to work with an orchestra and some very, very fine musicians. There was a drummer, Dave Mattacks, who played with Fairport Convention. The bass player, David Paton, was phenomenal; he was from The Bay City Rollers, just a fantastic bass player. It gave me a chance to really work to the visual thing; that's why I did it.

I thought to myself, 'that was me…'. It's always a great feeling when you're praised by someone of the stature of Jimmy Page.

1982. Camel

Abbey Road was like a home from home for me now – I'd recorded more albums there than anywhere else.

In 1981 while recording *Eye in the Sky* with The Alan Parsons Project in Studio Two, I met Andy Latimer in the canteen and he told me that Camel were recording an album in Studio Three. Andy asked if I was available to record with them. I told him I'd love to work with Camel, but I had my commitments to The Project and I was more or less booked up solid for the next two months.

We struck up a good friendship and I'd pop along to Studio Three whenever I was free to listen to Camel recordings. Andy contacted me again at the end of the year and asked if I'd be free to work on his next album, *The Single Factor.* The album was so named because Decca records had asked Andy to write chart material. Decca wanted singles and chart success. Camel were always an album band to my ears, in the same way as Yes, King Crimson and early Genesis were, so I'm not surprised that Andy was a bit pissed off at their suggestion.

The recordings for *The Single Factor* took place in Abbey Road Studio Three during the months of January and February 1982. The first song to be recorded was 'Sasquatch', a lively instrumental which features Simon Phillips on drums, who has played with The Who, Jeff Beck and Toto, myself on bass, Peter Bardens on organ and Andrew Latimer himself on guitar. Peter and I would work together on the Keats album, but more on that later.

The sessions went really well and I was enjoying working with the musicians and producer Tony Clarke, with Haydn Bendall as engineer. Haydn was actively involved in the work with The Project, so we knew each other pretty well. Andy mentioned a tour starting in May 1982 and he asked me if I was available, but Mary was pregnant at this time, she was due in April 1982 and I wasn't sure if it would be possible to take on the rehearsals and tour at that time. I wanted to be at home for the month of April and I explained this to Andy. But he said that he could arrange for rehearsals to take place in Edinburgh. It sounded like I could probably do this tour and I had been doing a lot of studio work, so touring would be a welcome change. I discussed it with Mary and if she had been unsure about it, I would have turned it down. She was happy to hear that the rehearsals could take place locally and said she was fine about me doing the tour. I suggested to Andy that we try to book Heartbeat studios which is located ten miles from Edinburgh in the North Middleton area. The studio is owned by my good friend Davie Valentine and had only been in operation for a couple of months at the time. All was arranged and Andy would stay with Mary and I for the duration of the rehearsals. We could tell from day one that this was going to be a fun tour. Heartbeat is located in an outbuilding within the grounds of a dairy farm; it was really refreshing to drive out to the country to start running through the songs and planning the set.

Kathryn Susan Paton was born on May 6, 1982. She was late; in fact, I think she was about ten days late, which caused a little anxiety regarding the tour start date, but all was fine and Mary and I had another beautiful baby daughter.

The tour began on the May 16 at Liverpool Empire theatre turned out to be a really fun one, not only for me but for Andy too. *www.camelproductions.com* described the line-up:

> The mix of personalities was magical, with a ceaseless, positive energy from Chris Rainbow who, with Paton and Tosh (Scotsmen, all three), maintained a flow of laughter from start to finish of the tour'. Kit Watkins (keyboards) had returned for his third Camel tour and the level of musicianship delighted audiences. Latimer would call it 'the funniest tour I've ever been on'.

Andy Ward had been the original drummer for Camel, but there were many problems with his health, including a self-inflicted hand injury, so Camel needed a drummer. I had managed to convince Andy that Stuart Tosh could handle the gig. Playing with Camel is pretty demanding for any drummer, but I'm happy to say that Stuart handled the intricacies very well.

We did have a magical time on that tour, and I only have happy memories of our travels and gigs. There was a great feeling of comradery and compatibility with that version of the band.

1983. The Move to England.

I'd been in Abbey Road recording the *Eye in the Sky* album. It was wintertime and a nice crisp morning when I left London for my drive back home to Edinburgh. I was driving a BMW 316. They were notoriously light in the rear and I did notice that I'd get stuck or lose traction in the snow while other cars seemed to handle the conditions without too much of a problem. In fact, Mary's Honda Civic held the road extremely well compared to the BMW. The journey from London to Edinburgh is usually around eight hours, so it was dark by the time I reached the Scottish border. My drive took me up the M6, which merged into the A74 at Gretna Green. It was then a short 40-minute drive east along the A702 into Edinburgh. I'd made that drive so many times it was becoming tedious; it was never a drive I looked forward to.

As we drove, I didn't realise that the temperature had fallen quite sharply on the journey north. As I drove out of the town of Bigger, I accelerated to the 60-mile-per-hour limit. I eased my foot off the accelerator as I approached a slight bend in the road and without warning, the car just spun out of control. I didn't have any time to react and before I knew it, the car had rolled over a couple of times and ended up in a field on its four wheels. I was in shock and the bag that had been on the passenger seat had shot out through the rear window. It took me a few minutes to get over the initial reaction and my elbow hurt a little, but apart from that, I was OK. I had to kick the passenger door open to get out. The car was a write-off and one of the wheels was totally shattered.

I picked up my bag and headed towards a farmhouse that I could see on the brow of the hill. A slightly nervous-looking farmer answered my knock on the door and I explained my accident to him. He very kindly invited me into the house and his wife made a fuss of me as soon as she was told what had happened. She could see how shocked and shaken I was and offered to me a cup of tea. When she handed me the cup, I couldn't stop my hand from shaking. They said I should sit for a while till I calmed down then I could use the telephone. After a few minutes, I felt calm enough to telephone the AA for a recovery truck. I also called Mary and told her I'd be a little late as I'd had a flat tyre and would need to wait for the AA. I didn't see any point in alarming her. The recovery truck arrived an hour later and pulled my car from the field, then drove me to my house. But Mary guessed that I'd had an accident, so it was then that we discussed moving to England. It seemed inevitable now.

We drove down to Berkshire to start house hunting and stayed with my sister, who lived in a newly built house in Winnersh, just a mile from Wokingham. Our intention was to start looking in the Maidenhead area, but after viewing a few houses, we were a little disappointed in what we saw, so we drove back to Winnersh and explained to Nina that we didn't want to move there. Nina said we should have a word with the site agents for Nina's estate in Winnersh as she thought they might have other homes available in the area. The builders had just finished their building work, but the site agent still had a hut on the estate, so we wondered round and asked if any of the houses were still available. He said they'd all been taken, but it looked like one had just fallen through and if we were quick, we could drive up to the site office in Wokingham and leave a deposit on that property. He gave us the keys to 2 Eastbury Park and told us to have a good look at the house and then drop the keys back before heading into Wokingham to give a deposit. We really liked the house – it seemed ideal. So that's how we ended up living in Winnersh, just around the corner from my sister. It then took a couple of months for us to sell up in Edinburgh and make the move to Berkshire.

1983 was a busy one and I was happy that my journey time to London was a mere 40 minutes and not eight hours.

One of the first albums I worked on after moving south was *Andrew Powell and The Philharmonia Orchestra Play the best of The Alan Parsons Project*, another Abbey Road recording. That was followed by *Ammonia Avenue,* with The Alan Parsons Project. Another Camel album was recorded at the end of 1983, which was *Stationary Traveller*, recorded at Riverside Studios, England. In December 1983, we began recording the *Keats* album again in Abbey Road.

1984. Keats

An offshoot of The Alan Parsons Project was the group Keats. It featured Ian Bairnson, Stuart Elliott, and vocalist Colin Blunstone from The

Zombies, who often featured on APP albums. Added to the mix was Peter Bardens, formerly of Camel on keyboards and me on bass. This band was another concept of Eric's. It was a great idea and a great pleasure for me to be working with Colin as I am a big fan of his work and I love his voice. We signed to EMI and released an album entitled *Keats*, produced by Alan Parsons.

It came about as Eric Woolfson asked for a meeting with the core Project band – Ian, Stuart and myself. He put forward the idea of forming a band for another project, and he also wanted to include Colin Blunstone and Peter Bardens. I'd met Peter on the recording of the Camel album *The Single Factor* and I am a great Zombies fan so I was delighted at the idea of being in a band with Colin. We were all very receptive to Eric's idea and he told us that Alan Parsons was already keen to be involved in the production. We agree to meet with Peter and Colin and have a play together.

We all had songs and were eager to get into rehearsals. Lots of ideas were coming together and there were some really good completed songs from Peter. Stuart and Colin were writing good songs together too.

We rehearsed at Putney Bridge under the Arches. It was exciting and the music was strong and powerful. This would be another Abbey Road recording using Studios Two and Three. Richard Cottle was brought on board as well and provided additional keyboard parts, as well as saxophone and synthesizers. I really thought that Keats would attract a lot of attention, but it didn't make as much of an impact as we all expected. 'Turn Your Heart Around' was the initial single release. It's a Peter Bardens song and, tonally, very much in the Asia, Boston and Ambrosia bracket. It had that American supergroup sound and we all agreed that it was the ideal single, representing perfectly what Keats were all about. We were classified as a progressive rock band, which suited us fine.

I wish more had come of Keats. I suppose we were not focused enough after the disappointing reaction to our album release. We all had other things going on and the whole concept was not organic enough for it to have staying power. Keats just slowly fizzled out and faded away. The album still stands up well to this day and has become a bit of a collector's item.

Elton John

It was 1985, and although I didn't know it at the time, I'd recorded *Stereotomy*, my last album with The Alan Parsons Project. That brought to an end my run of nine consecutive recordings. That final album recording took place at Mayfair Studios between October 1984 and August 1985. Both Alan and Eric said that the record suffered from a lack of label support but *Stereotomy* earned a Grammy nomination in 1987 for Best Rock Instrumental Performance – Orchestra, Group, or Soloist – for the track 'Where's the Walrus?'

1985 was another busy year for me. I'd been asked to play bass for many different artists and I was really enjoying my role as a session musician. It was a pretty good job and I was very comfortable working behind the scenes with a variety of different artists and musical styles. By this time, I'd worked with David Courtney (with Geoff Emerick engineering), Paul McCartney, on Don Black's *Dear Anyone*, Kate Bush, Chris De Burgh, Chris Rea, Elaine Paige, Jimmy Page and Camel. Oh, and Pilot, of course.

I received a call asking about my availability for a three-day session. I was available for the dates mentioned and I asked which studio – it was Sol Studios, Cookham. It would be a midday start. All was agreed and I finally asked who the artist was. It was Elton John!

I was absolutely delighted to hear that I'd be playing on an Elton John album. It really threw me because only a couple of weeks before that phone call, I'd had a dream about Elton, and it was very vivid. Elton was pursuing me over various obstacles. For some reason, I was jumping over walls and Elton was behind me, climbing and jumping and pursuing me from wall to wall. It was a happy dream, a bit like we were playing a game of some kind. So that is why I was really surprised to hear that I was going to be recording with Elton.

The day arrived for the session. Cookham is a short drive from where we lived in Wokingham, so I got there within 20 minutes. I took my basses from the boot of the car and walked toward the main entrance to the studio. I had to pause for a moment and take a deep breath before I plucked up the courage to open the door. Dave Mattacks was already setting up his kit as I loaded the rest of my gear in. I was leaning over the drum booth when I could see Dave smiling and looking slightly to my right. I felt a presence beside me and looked round to see Elton standing just an arm's length from me. He said, 'Hello, Davie Paton' and he shook my hand as I said, 'nice to meet you Elton'. Dave had obviously met Elton before and the three of us chatted a little until Dave said he was just going to grab a coffee before we got started and I said that I'd set up my basses.

Elton stayed in the studio with me and we talked about the studio and the album he was recording. I picked up my fretless Musicman Stingray fretless bass just to give it a tune-up. Meanwhile, Elton sat at the piano and started to play a sequence of chords. They didn't sound familiar and I reckoned it was probably a song he was going to be recording for the album. I thought it would be a good idea to play along with him, as he probably wanted to hear what I could do. We played around the sequence, occasionally making eye contact and he looked happy with what I was playing. We probably played through the chord sequence three or four times and I was getting familiar with it. Eventually, Elton stopped playing and said to me, 'That's really good; I think you have the gist of it and it's the first song we'll be recording today; it's called 'Nikita'. He walked to the control room and told Gus Dudgeon and the band he was ready to start. Into the studio walked Nik Kershaw (guitar), Fred Mandel (keyboards) and Dave Mattacks.

Elton introduced Nick as 'Nikita' Kershaw, he loved having alternative names for people, and I became 'Gypsy Jock' during the photo shoot for the following year's *Leather Jackets* album. The makeup department stuck false sideburns on me and I sat posing on a motorbike, trying to look tough. At one point, fellow Scot, the comedian Billy Connolly remarked, 'you look like the Disneyland chapter of the Hells Angels'. Continuing the theme of using humorous false names, when on tour, Elton would sometimes have his hotel room booked under the name 'Lord Choc Ice'.

The recording of 'Nikita' went really well. Elton was delighted and complimented me on capturing the essence of the song. I hadn't intended to play fretless bass on it, but that's the way it worked out because I was tuning it when he sat down at the piano. Elton was always friendly and helped me feel at ease. It can be quite nerve-wracking working with an idol and I know he could sense that I was slightly overwhelmed. In the end, there were two more songs that I was asked to play on 'Candy By The Pound' and 'Tell Me What The Papers Say'.

Here's some information on the album. *Ice on Fire* was the nineteenth studio album by Elton John. Recorded at Sol Studios and released in November 1985, it was his first album since *Blue Moves* to be produced by his original long-time producer, Gus Dudgeon, while myself and Charlie Morgan appeared for the first time on bass and drums respectively, replacing original band members Dee Murray and Nigel Olsson. Fred

Mandel, who had played with Elton during the *Breaking Hearts* tour, also contributed guitar and keyboards. The album was met with little praise and only reached Number 48 on the US charts, although it reached Number three in the UK. 'Nikita' and 'Wrap Her Up' became top 20 hits, the latter reaching number 20 in the US, and the former reached number seven in the US and number three in the UK. In the US, the album was certified gold in June 1986 by the RIAA.

'Do They Know It's Christmas?' is a charity song written in 1984 by Bob Geldof and Midge Ure to raise money for the famine in Ethiopia. It was released in the United Kingdom on 3 December 1984. It entered the UK singles chart at number one and stayed there for five weeks. It sold a million copies in the first week, becoming the fastest-selling single in UK chart history and it held this title until 1997, when it was overtaken by Elton John's 'Candle in the Wind 1997'. UK sales exceeded three million on New Years' Eve, 1984. News of the follow-up Live Aid concert was all over the media and Elton had been asked to perform but it was John Reid who told me that Elton would like me to be the bass player for that gig.

We started rehearsals for Live Aid at Elstree Studios and during the rehearsals, Davey Johnstone mentioned a world tour and asked if I'd be interested in that. I couldn't believe what I was hearing. I was so ready to get out on the road, and to tour with Elton was a dream come true. I was sitting at the side of the stage in Elstree when I noticed Elton arrive with George Michael. They were at the back of the studio chatting and Elton was pointing my way. The next thing I knew, George started to walk towards me; he was smiling and said, 'Hello David, nice to meet you. I just wanted you to know that 'January' had a huge influence on me and I love the song'. I didn't know what to say, I mumbled something about how special 'Careless Whisper' was, but he insisted that 'January' was wonderful and very special to him.

Elton called me and invited me to a playback of *Ice on Fire*. He said, 'bring your wife, Mary'. The playback was held in the control room of The Sol Studios and there were many celebs there, including the guys from Queen. We listened to the tracks and after 'Nikita' was played, Elton stopped the playback and said to everyone, 'please give a big hand to David Paton for that wonderful bass playing', Brian May shook my hand and said 'that was you? Well done, that's excellent'.

After the playback, Elton came over to Mary and me and said he wanted to talk to us in private. He spoke to Mary and told her he was doing the world tour and wanted to make sure that she was ok with it; after all, we'd probably be away for the best part of a year. Mary said, 'take him, he loves touring and I know he'll be well looked after'. With that, Elton told Mary she would be welcome to join me on the tour at any point.

A few days later, I received a call from Eric Woolfson, saying that he would be starting the recording of the next Alan Parsons Project album and he began to name the dates. I had to stop him and tell him I couldn't be involved because I was now with The Elton John Band. He was not happy at all. All he said was, 'well, thank you very much' in an angry tone and ended the conversation with that.

But it was now time to start rehearsals for the world tour. I felt on top of the world. All I had to do was play, and I *love* playing my bass. I had no-one telling me what to do and I was well rehearsed as I knew most of the songs before I even got the set list, so I was very comfortable with the set. I was a very happy bunny. Rehearsing all the wonderful Elton John songs with the full band was fantastic; everyone had nailed the arrangements and it was a big, powerful sound on stage – and it was loud!

Clive Franks is Elton's out-front sound engineer. He has been with Elton since the early 1970s and he worked at Dick James music as a studio sound engineer before then. He's a very funny guy with a great sense of humour. If you're old enough to remember the Troggs tapes, Clive was the guy who put the two-track Studer into record to capture a day in the studio with The Troggs. That recording is now legendary amongst musicians – it's hilarious stuff.

We were discussing cars one day when Clive mentioned the time when he was invited to dinner at Elton's house and the subject there got around to cars. There were a few people at the dinner and Clive was asked what his all-time favourite car was. He said he loved the Mercedes SL convertible. They all discussed cars for a while then the subject moved on to something else. A few months later, Clive was back at Elton's having dinner. It was Clive's birthday and he was delighted that Elton had a dinner party on this special day. Everyone wished Clive a happy birthday and Elton leaned over the table and laid a set of car keys in front of him. He gathered everyone together and they all walked out the front door to see a brand-new white Mercedes SL in the driveway. Elton said, 'It's all yours, Clive. Happy birthday'.

Elton is a very generous man; he was always making donations to charity and giving gifts to the band. When portable CD players arrived, he presented the band with one each and a set of headphones. I remember him reading a book by John Train called *Most Remarkable Names*. It's a very entertaining book with some stories, a few caricatures and pages and pages of people's names and their home town. For example:

Cheatham & Steele, Bankers, Oregon.
Dennis Elbow, Fisherman, New York.
Dr & Dr Doctor, Connecticut.
Dr Fealey, gynaecologist, Florida.

It's such a funny book and all the names are genuine. Elton signed the book 'To Gypsy Jock, with love, Elton' and gave it to me. These gifts were very special from a man who really cared and loved to give gifts and see the joy on the recipient's face.

Saturday, July 13, 1985. Live Aid.

The excitement was growing, and talk of Live Aid was everywhere. Elton was doing TV and radio interviews announcing his new band and talking about his upcoming world tour. July 12 was a sleepless night. The Paton family woke early and the house was full of excitement.

Status Quo appeared on stage at midday with their opening song, 'Rockin' All Over the World'. As we watched it on TV at home, I found it hard to believe I'd be there on stage with Elton that evening.

A limousine arrived late afternoon and took Mary and me to London, where we met up with the band and were driven to Wembley by private bus. There were 13 of us and we were joined by Billy Connolly, Pamela Stephenson, Kiki Dee and by members of the John Reid organisation. When we arrived, we were taken to our dressing room area and then invited to a VIP area to watch David Bowie perform his set.

I can't really put into words the excitement and atmosphere in the stadium, it really was an amazing event. There were 72000 people there and the roar of the crowd was almost deafening. They were drowning out the stage sound! Now, if you're a musician and you've been to a big event like this, you'll know that when you watch other performers, you just get eager to get up there and play. I was like that. I was going on stage with Elton John and I just couldn't wait to play my bass in front of this massive crowd.

The dressing room area was set out within a huge circle with tables and chairs and parasols in the centre. I saw Paul and Linda McCartney arrive to a huge flurry of activity. Many bands and solo artists were sitting at the tables and chatting. It was a great thing to see your heroes all mixing, laughing, chatting and relaxing in the sun. The time was drawing near for Elton to take the stage and I'd be lying if I said I wasn't nervous. Ha, I have heard it said that if you don't get nervous before a performance, your heart is really not in it and I'd agree with that. We were all pacing about, waiting for Nick or Bazz, the tour managers, to appear and say, 'right guys, you're on'.

And then it happened, and we were on stage hearing the opening chords to 'I'm Still Standing'. I couldn't wipe the smile off my face. It wasn't just happiness that I felt – the whole thing was an emotional experience. I thought to myself that we were here to help feed the world and millions of people were together to support this amazing event.

1.5 billion people watched on TV and if I'm ever asked 'what's the biggest audience I've ever played to', I always give the same answer. It was Live Aid.

1985 and 1986. Elton John Ice On fire Tour

It was now time to start rehearsals for the world tour and time for the band to get to know each other:

It was a big band:

Elton: lead vocals, piano
Davey Johnstone: lead guitar, backing vocals
David Paton: bass guitar
Fred Mandel: keyboards, rhythm guitar
Charlie Morgan: drums
Ray Cooper: percussion (UK leg)
Jody Linscott: percussion (Europe and North America legs)
Alan Carvell: backing vocals
Helena Springs: backing vocals
Shirley Lewis: backing vocals
David Bitelli: Saxophone
Rick Taylor: Trombone
Paul Spong: Trumpet
Raul D'Olevera: Trumpet

I thought back to the times that Billy Lyall and I would sit and listen to *Madman Across The Water*, totally enthralled. Now, here I was in the band.

Rehearsals took place at Elstree Studios for a week.

Playing all the wonderful Elton John songs was heaven and I didn't want it to stop. I've always had good friendships with drummers in bands and this happened with Charlie Morgan. We shared similar interests – cars, technology and cameras. We both decided to buy video cameras and proceeded to video everything we were doing. Elton didn't seem to mind, so we managed to collect a large amount of footage on the world tour.

On 14 November 1985, the *Ice On Fire* tour began in Dublin and continued across the British Isles, including nine nights at Wembley Arena before concluding on January 11 1986, in Belfast, Northern Ireland. As usual, Elton selected a few of the songs from his most recent album to include in the set; in this instance, 'Shoot Down the Moon', 'This Town' and the singles 'Nikita' and 'Wrap Her Up'.

We all met many famous faces throughout the tour and in particular during the London dates. Rod Stewart was backstage chatting and laughing with the band and he walked with us to the stage and clapped us on with words of encouragement. Every show was a knockout as the audiences were so receptive and created such a great atmosphere. One evening before the show, we were asked to join Elton in his dressing room. It was a huge surprise for us all to be introduced one by one to Princess Diana. She shook hands with all of us, and in true Scottish style, I remember giving her a fairly firm handshake.

After the show, I walked along to the green room and was surprised to see that it was packed with celebrities. I made my way to the buffet area and noticed Princess Diana leaning forward to spear a couple of olives with a cocktail stick. I took a plate and picked up a couple of sandwiches. When I turned around, I was face to face with George Harrison. He started to talk to me and I didn't know what to say. I couldn't bring anything to mind except, 'oh fuck, that's George Harrison'. He was telling me how much he enjoyed my bass playing, but I was dumbstruck and could hardly put a sentence together. I only remember thanking him and walking away. Of course, I kick myself now as I realise that he wanted to talk in more depth.

The tour included a gig in Edinburgh. At that time, my Dad worked for the city council and was based in Market Street. One job my Dad had was to unlock the doors to the various departments in the city chambers. He told me that he unlocked the library door and walked in to turn the light on. He said he noticed a lady dressed very elegantly in what he described as Victorian clothing. She was standing with her back to a window and reading a book. Without really thinking about it, he said good morning and walked out of the room. Then he thought, wait a minute, how did she get in there? He walked back to the library and she was gone. He couldn't find an explanation for that event.

Dad asked me if Elton would be interested in visiting Mary King's Close. At that time in 1986, the close was not open to the public as it is now, so it would be a real treat to visit. This is a historic area located underground below the Royal Mile in Edinburgh. It took its name from Mary King, who lived in the Close in the 17th century. It was originally a web of narrow side streets called closes which led off the Royal Mile. They could be locked up at each end at night to keep the undesirables out. The close was bricked up during the great plague of 1645, with up to 300 (presumably) infected residents left to die in their homes. Mary King's Close is now a visitor attraction where guests can take guided tours and learn about Edinburgh's hidden history and, a few years ago, a Japanese psychic claimed to have met a young girl called Annie in one of the rooms. She's said to be a plague victim abandoned by her parents. The psychic said she wanted a doll to stop her feeling so lonely. Since then, visitors from around the world have donated toys for her, and a pile of dolls and teddies has built up in 'Annie's Room'.

When I mentioned Mary King's Close to Elton, he was keen to visit, and percussionist Ray Cooper was particularly keen as, with his Hand Made Films connection (he was formerly head of production there), he thought the area would be a great location for a film. A private tour was arranged, and I was asked to accompany Elton from his hotel to the location. Elton stayed at the Waldorf Astoria in the West End of Edinburgh, where he had a suite on the top floor with fantastic views of the castle.

A limousine drove us to the City Chambers. We arrived to be greeted by the Lord Provost and a few dignitaries. My Mum and Dad were there and Elton was happy to meet them and pose for a few photos.

Edinburgh is a really buzzing city, especially around the West End and the High Street. We entered the close through a small door to an area that was being used by workmen to store ladders and paint. As I said, Mary Kings Close was not open to the public at that time, but we did have a tour guide who was very familiar with the route to take through the underground streets. We walked through the storage area and down a few flights of steep stairs. There was no door at the bottom of the stairs and we were amazed to walk out onto a cobbled street with a metal handrail on the wall, as there was quite a gradient. The street was dimly lit with temporary lighting and this only helped add to the eery atmosphere. There was an overpass a couple of stories above us with a window looking down onto the street below. We walked up the street to a butcher's shop. The butcher's sign was still visible above the door and as we walked through to the back of the shop, we could see hooks in the ceiling where the butcher would hang the animal carcasses. This really brought it home what life would have been like in 16th-century Edinburgh.

It was a real pleasure to be in Edinburgh with Elton and the tour around Mary King's close was an added bonus. The gig in the evening at the Playhouse was a huge success and it was wonderful to be introduced by Elton as 'Edinburgh's own Davie Paton'.

After the UK leg of the tour, we went on to Spain, France, Switzerland, Germany, Austria, Netherlands and finished the European dates in Belgium on April 26 1986. We had a couple of months off before the start of the USA tour and that gave me some quality time at home with my family.

I had a call from Elton asking if I was free to play bass for him on a few new songs he was writing at home. It was only a 20-minute drive from my house, and when I arrived, he was busy at the piano finishing off another composition. That was Elton, every time I arrived to work with him; he was sitting at the piano composing. When I left at night, he'd still be at the piano, working on a new song. He always had so much enthusiasm and it was inspiring to watch him working.

Charlie Morgan arrived and we soon set up and started working on the songs together. Renate (Elton's then-wife) was there helping out with engineering and production, and Adrian, who looked after technical matters in the studio was also there. I got chatting with Renate. She loved being in the studio and wanted to do more studio work, so she asked me if I had any new songs. I hadn't been writing but told her I could get some songs together and would be happy to work with her. She was a very well-qualified sound engineer, and although nothing came of the recordings, it was fun for her to continue doing what she loved and I was happy to have her engineer and co-produce my own songs.

Harpo Marx?

Elton's singing voice had been playing up quite a bit and by the time we started the USA tour, it was noticeable that he had developed a bit of a growl. We were in New York. I'd finished breakfast and was preparing to do a bit of sightseeing when I received a call from Renate. She asked me to come up to their apartment on the top floor and to bring my video camera with me. I didn't know what to expect! I knocked on the door.

Elton answered, and he was dressed as Harpo Marx! It was the complete Harpo get-up of blond, curly wig, trench coat, top hat, scarf and he was carrying a klaxon horn. He also had an Etch-a-Sketch and he wrote on it, 'I mustn't speak, I have nodules on my vocal cords and need to rest my voice'. He asked me to video him and follow him through the hotel. He had a list of people rooming on the tour and we walked along the hotel corridors to find rooms on the list. There were a few surprised faces when they answered their door and I'm not sure that they recognised Elton at all, as it really was a very convincing costume. After the fun, we made our way back to Elton's apartments. I remarked on the view from them and Elton wrote on the Etch-a-Sketch 'follow me'. I followed him through the apartment until we came to an elevator. The elevator took us up and onto the roof of the hotel, Where we had a panoramic view of Manhattan Island. He'd left his Etch-a-Sketch downstairs and was pointing out the landmarks and writing it on the lead surround of the waist-high wall with his finger. 'Chrysler Building'. 'Empire State'. It was quite a surreal experience.

1986. Texas

During my school days, I was aware of some folk who'd visit England for a week and come back to school with an English accent. It probably lasted an hour or two until they realised that nobody was impressed and we realised that they just wanted to be the centre of attention.

I remember being in Texas for an openair concert with Elton. As we stood on stage for a sound check, I saw a police car approaching along a track road. The dust was billowing out from behind the car as it bumped its way along the track and it looked like something from a movie. The car pulled up at the side of the stage and I watched the sheriff get out. He was a big guy, wearing sunglasses, smoking a cigar and he placed a Stetson on his head as he exited his vehicle. I thought, 'Wow! This is impressive; I'm really in Texas now'. He walked to the front of the stage, looked up at me and said, 'Are yi awright there, pal? Where're the Scottish guys in the band, then?' He'd been in Texas for 30 years and had the broadest Glasgow accent.

The tour of the USA started on August 17, 1986. We played many cities in USA and Canada, east coast to the west coast. New York was our base for many dates in the east. We'd fly back and forward to places within a reasonable distance from there. We'd come off stage after the concert, get straight onto the bus and then we'd drive directly to the plane on the runway. There was a passport check but no real hassle. After our final show in Los Angeles, we were told that there would be an after-show party in the Cartier shop on Rodeo Drive. Mary and I made our way there with Fred Mandel and his wife, Paula. On arrival, we were introduced (by Elton) to many well-known celebrities. Sylvester Stallone and his wife Brigitte Nielsen looked particularly impressive. You get a bit of a shock seeing a movie star of that stature in the flesh.

John Reid came over to me and said, 'I want to introduce you to my friend Bob'. We all shook hands and he started talking 'bass' to me. He said that the bass was very clear during the concert and he could hear every note. So, I was looking and listening to Bob and it suddenly dawned on me that I was talking to Robert Wagner! We found a table and we all sat down and had a great conversation about music and movies. I always got a thrill out of meeting people I've admired and I was excited that Elton made a point of introducing us to them. It could be Joan Collins, Billy Jean King or Patricia Arquette. Christ, I even met Roy Orbison!

The tour finished in Los Angeles on October 15 1986.

We had a three-week break before the start of the Australian tour. I was informed that I could fly back home or stay on in Los Angeles if I wanted to. It seemed like a good idea to ask Mary, Sarah and Katy if they wanted to fly over and stay with me in Los Angeles for the break, so that's what happened. They flew out a few days before the end of the tour and we stayed on at the same hotel I'd been staying at, with the hotel providing a limo to take me to the airport to meet them. I rented a car and we really had a great time visiting Disneyland, Universal Studios, Howard Hughes' plane The Spruce Goose and The Queen Mary. We visited Fred Mandel, who lived just outside LA and Davey Johnstone invited us to his place in the Hollywood Hills. There was never a dull moment.

1986. Elton John Tour De Force, Australia

From November 5 to December 14, 1986, Elton toured Australia with his 14-member band. The big bonus was having the 88-piece Melbourne Symphony Orchestra (MSO) and conductor James Newton Howard with us.

I'd never toured with an orchestra before and it was going to be challenging, especially for Clive Franks, who was at the desk taking care of the out-front sound. He was joined by Gus Dudgeon, who took care of the orchestral balance. Gus was in a mobile studio back stage and he did a sub-mix of the whole orchestra. That was sent as a stereo mix to Clive at the front-of-house desk.

I'm sure it was just as much a challenge for the orchestra as it was for us. We heard that some of the orchestral players were reluctant to be involved in a rock show, but after the first day's rehearsal, we realised that they were all converts to the music of Elton. It really was beautiful listening to the set that Elton played with just the orchestra; it was stunning. There were a few songs added to the set that we hadn't played live together, so we were all highly focused.

The Tour De Force began with three dates in Brisbane Entertainment centre, then nine dates in Melbourne Entertainment centre, one gig in Adelaide and two in Perth. We finished on December 14 with 13 nights at the Sydney Entertainment centre.

It was hard to believe that we'd been touring for a year – it had flown by like a whirlwind and I didn't want it to stop. There had never been a bad gig for me with Elton and I loved every second of it. But here we were at the end of a musical dream.

Elton needed to get his nodules removed from his vocal cords.

This is what Fred Mandel and Charlie Morgan have to say about the tour to *EJ.com*:

> Fred Mandel: He was getting vocal nodes. I remember when he came out and talked to us and he was saying, 'I think I have throat cancer.' He was very worried.
>
> Charlie Morgan: He had the operation the day after the last show.
>
> Fred Mandel: It turned out to be vocal nodes. I'll tell you, he certainly soldiered on through that. And I mean, Elton singing with nodes is better than a lot of people. At his worst, he still is a pretty damn good singer.
>
> Charlie Morgan: I do have a very vivid memory. We are playing 'Don't Let The Sun Go Down On Me' and I look over at Elton and I realise that there are tears streaming down his face as he's singing the chorus. I think that the thought that he was going into hospital and didn't know what the hell was going on was…
>
> Fred Mandel: … he thought it might be the last time he would sing that song.
>
> Charlie Morgan: It was really hitting him. When I looked over, it wasn't sweat, it was tears.
>
> Fred Mandel: He was in tears when he came and told us he thought it might be cancer. I actually think it was a pretty incredible thing that he was able to soldier on through that because that would be a psychological roadblock for a lot of people.

> Charlie Morgan: And for 26 shows! You think about that … that's pretty awesome, really.
> Fred Mandel: And [the band] weren't on for the whole time. But he was onstage from beginning to end for three-and-a-half hours. It's a big problem for any artist to do an hour and a half to two hours. Not only that, but you've got to stick to the arrangements. You can't just turn around, 'Ok guys, let's jam. String section, take it!' It doesn't work like that.
> Charlie Morgan: He was basically getting his voice back in shape in the middle of 'One Horse Town' each night. He was getting the phlegm out of his voice.

1988. Elton Takes Time Out.

We were recording *Reg Strikes Back* in Air Studios, Oxford Circus. I arrived early and was surprised to see Elton in the studio at the piano. He saw me and gestured for me to join him. He was writing a song around a lyric that Bernie had sent him. It was called 'Poor Cow'. He was very excited about it and asked me to sit down and listen. Wow, what a fabulous song. I was mesmerized. He finished playing and looked at me. I said, 'It's wonderful, Elton, it's all there'. He said he needed another verse. We walked back into the control room and he asked someone to get Bernie on the phone. Bernie was in LA and it was 2:30 pm in the UK, so it would have been very early in the morning on the West Coast. Someone managed to reach Bernie and I could hear Elton talking to him. He was telling Bernie he needed another verse for the lyric. The next thing, Elton was snapping his fingers and saying, 'pen, pen'. He got the pen and started writing. I heard him say, 'thanks Bernie, that's great'. With that, he turned to me and said, 'it's complete now, so we'll record this when the rest of the guys get here'. I was astonished. Bernie had given Elton another verse over the phone and it was created instantly. It was probably 8:30 am, but he still managed to come up with a verse for a song he'd sent Elton probably a couple of weeks before we got to the studio.

But later, John Reid gathered the band together and told us that Elton would need a year out. The band were told that Elton would be in touch but that he needed the year out to get himself together. That was very disappointing news but understandable.

We all got on with our lives and I lost touch with the rest of the guys in the band.

I remember feeling a bit lost when that dream came to an end. I'd come out of one of the best times of my life and fell down to earth with a bump.

All the opportunities I'd had before joining Elton were now gone, I'd been out of the session scene for three years and my place had been taken by other players. I was out of work and feeling down.

Have you ever been down and you think that you can't go any further down? That's how I felt. Christ! Even my petrol lawn mower packed in as I was cutting the grass, and I felt like I was going through a period of very bad luck. I needed to get back to work.

I asked Mary if she would consider emigrating to Australia. We gave it a lot of thought and discussed it regularly. I applied for immigration to the Australian immigration Authority, but I quickly found out that I didn't need to go through the points system and could apply as an entertainer and in the end, Mary and I were both accepted. We booked flights to Sydney and I planned to approach record companies to try to reboot my solo career. We had a really great time in Sydney and became quite serious about making the move.

I made appointments with a couple of record companies and I became optimistic about getting some interest in my career. But it didn't quite go as planned and I was told that most record companies in Sydney were promoting US and UK artists who were signed to British or American labels. They said I'd have a better chance of signing with a UK company than an Australian subsidiary. That was disappointing news and dented our hopes of starting a new life in Australia.

We visited a club that evening and got into conversation with a few of the local musicians. They all said the same thing to me; I'd have more opportunities in the UK than I would in Australia. We made our way back to the UK, knowing that we had to return to Australia within three months to renew the visas. Now we were in two minds about making the move. But things started to go well when we returned home, and the unlucky times were beginning to lift.

Rick Wakeman, Fish and Recording Other Artists

1988. Rick Wakeman

It was late 1987 and I was still living in Berkshire. There was a studio nearby in Wraysbury owned by a Scotsman by the name of Brian Adams (not *that* Bryan Adams). Brian was a bit of a wide boy, a bit of a Jack the lad, but a likeable rogue. He managed Rick as well as Denny Laine. Denny had previously sung with the Moody Blues, with the hit 'Go Now' and he was also in Paul McCartney's band Wings, co-writing 'Mull of Kintyre', which I'd sung on over ten years previously.

I was asked along to the studio to do a bass session for Rick. When I arrived, Rick was in the control room with John Burns, the in-house sound engineer. They were playing back a fairly complicated piece of music. We did our introductions and I instantly liked Rick, as he had a friendly and happy attitude. He asked if I'd be ok with the piece they just played, and I said I thought it was a bit of a challenge and I'd need to hear it a few more times before I'd be ready to start recording. He said, 'Ok, no problem, I'll leave you to it, give me a shout if you have any problems'. He disappeared into the studio and left John and me to get on with recording the bass.

Ricks methods for breaking the ice could be a little – shall we say – near the knuckle. But they did relieve any nervousness I felt, and I realised he wanted me to feel relaxed. A particular joke he told us about a hunter and a moose was very funny, but that's another story. Even though his humour was kind of basic, it made me laugh. John explained that despite his grumpy old man reputation, he was a bit of a joker.

When I'd completed the bass part, Rick came back to the control room and listened to the track. He was very enthusiastic about my playing and told me it was the perfect part for his composition. I was asked to get more involved with his musical projects, which I was happy to do. The album I was working on was *Time Machine* and I enjoyed this music better than the pieces I'd heard at a concert I went to of his five years earlier.

We had just finished rehearsing for a tour and dates were in the diary when I received a call from Charlie Morgan saying that Elton wanted to do a gig and asked me if I was interested. That put me in a very awkward position. I told Charlie I'd really be letting Rick down if I backed out of his tour, so my answer was no, I couldn't do it. I wish I'd had time to think it through before I gave my reply. I sacrificed a great opportunity because I didn't want to let Rick down. I really should have tried to find a solution. I've now learned to say, 'give me a day or two to get back to you'.

I didn't mention anything to Rick.

We started gigging as a band, The English Rock Ensemble. The band was Tony Fernandez (drums), Ashley Holt (vocals), Rick and myself, with occasionally Dzal Martin on guitar. It was great, I started to enjoy the complexity of the music and Tony and I were soon a well-locked rhythm section.

In 1990 we recorded the *African Bach* album. A South African company wanted Rick to record a video for them in Johannesburg, but I told Rick I couldn't do it because of Musicians Union Rules at that time. I called the MU and asked them about it, and I was told I'd be blacklisted if I performed in South Africa. Apartheid involved a system of racial segregation and white supremacy and placed all political power in the hands of a white minority. Queen played Sun City and were swiftly fined by the Musicians' Union. They were not alone: the likes of Rod Stewart and Status Quo also played Sun City, easing their consciences by making donations to local charities. So eventually, it was agreed that we would film in Swaziland instead.

It was my first time in Africa and I loved Swaziland, which is now known as the Kingdom of Eswatini. We were going to be sleeping in three-man tents, which sounded like a real adventure to me. But Dzal was having none of it – he slept in the van. Rick had a tent to himself at the end of a pathway which was dimly lit with a small oil lamp in the evening. Rick wouldn't walk down to his tent on his own and a ranger would usually accompany him. One time when the ranger wasn't available, I offered to walk with him, with me holding an oil lamp to help light the way. When we got to the tent, he took the lamp from me and said, 'thank you and good night'. I told him I needed it to get back. 'Goodnight, David', came the reply. I made my way back with just the light from the camp a 100 yards or so from Rick's tent. The next morning there was a lot of commotion coming from Rick's tent. There was squealing and yelling and stuff was being thrown about. First, a shoe came flying out, then a suitcase, then a warthog bolted out of one side and Rick came flying out the other. We could hardly move from laughing, but Rick was not quite so amused.

He wrote an album of music called *The Gospels* and was lucky enough to be offered a trip to Israel, where we would record live in an outdoor amphitheatre in Caesarea. Oh, the perks of the trade can lead to visiting some strange and interesting lands. The performance began at sunset and the backdrop was a tranquil beach. Rick was well dressed in a black suit and wing collar shirt with a sparkly bowtie. The story of Jesus was narrated by Robert Powell, adding another dimension to the musical performance. We performed with the Haifa Symphony Orchestra, the Eton College Chapel Choir and tenor Ramon Remedios, making the whole show a joy and and a complete success. It really was special and a great pleasure to be playing with the orchestra. The amphitheatre is in the capital of Roman Judea, and was the main venue of entertainment when Herod the Great was the ruler. It is a magnificent venue.

Rick lived on the Isle of Man and we started to record at his studio on the Isle. Norman Wisdom also lived there and he arrived at the studio while I was there. He was a naturally funny man and couldn't stop himself from falling into character. I loved being in his company – he'd made me laugh on so many occasions throughout my life.

I was contributing a lot to the recordings; Rick liked my guitar work as well as my bass playing, so I was doing a lot of that too. When he heard me play classical guitar, it must have planted a seed.

We finished a gig in Brighton and Rick spoke to me on the quiet. He said, 'Let's go for a walk as there's something I want to discuss with you'. We took a walk along the beachfront on a still evening with just the rumble of the surf on the beach. I had no idea what he wanted to talk about. He told me he wanted to do some concerts without the English Rock Ensemble. I thought he was going to say that I wouldn't be required for future gigs. He then started to explain that he'd like to perform with me as a duo. I was really surprised and delighted to hear that. He said that he wanted a more classical theme for his concerts; just me on bass and classical guitar and himself on keys. I liked the idea as I really enjoyed playing guitar in concert but to perform at such a level with Rick sounded like a real challenge. The logistics and the setting up were explained and I felt that I had to ask him about the fee I would receive as that was the only thing he didn't mention, but he said that it would remain the same as it currently was. I let him know I wasn't happy with that as my contribution would be a lot more than just bass player and in addition, he would be saving on expense by not having The English Rock Ensemble on the road. He pleaded poverty and said he couldn't afford to increase my fee and I made a joke about him owning a Rolls Royce. His answer was, 'you can be poor with a Rolls Royce in your garage'. So, I told him that his wage wouldn't sustain me and that I'd need to do extra work when it was offered to me. I suppose I felt let down after the sacrifices I'd made for him.

We did an enjoyable and successful tour playing the music from his *Classical Connections* album. We spent a lot of time together driving to gigs the length and breadth of England and Wales in his Rolls Royce. I remember being in a shopping mall with him, looking in a joke shop window. He turned to me and said, 'chase me', I said, 'what did you say?' He repeated, 'chase me'. With that, he took off and ran through the shopping mall with me chasing him, with both of us laughing our heads off and shoppers stopping to look at a tall, blond Rick Wakeman being chased by a short Scottish bass player.

Yes, we had a lot of laughs together. There were no fallings out, and it was a real pleasure to perform with such an accomplished player, a certain tightness with money not withstanding!

1990. Passions Cry

My Dad died in November 1989. That same year and just a month later, I was looking for music to play to bring in the New Year. I found a cassette tape I didn't recognise and put it on. I was amazed to hear my Dad sing 'Auld Lang Syne' at the press of the play button, it was a bit spooky and I felt that he was with me again for a few precious moments.

I wanted to record something in honour of my Dad as he was such a Robert Burns enthusiast. The idea came to me to record an album of traditional Scottish music. My friend John McNairn had played a few Border songs for me, and I really liked them. Songs like 'Jock o' Hazeldean' play really well on guitar and I learned a lot from just listening to John's interpretations, so I found a Robert Burns poem that I really liked and decided to write some music to it. The music worked well with the poem 'Count the Lawin'. I found another poem I really liked called 'The Holy Fair' and I also added music to that. I was getting back into the swing of writing again and started to enjoy it. Dad's favourite Burns song was 'Ae Fond Kiss' and I had to record the song even though I knew I'd never sing it as well as my Dad did. When I heard the Corries sing 'The Bonnie Blue Bonnets', I knew I could use that. I asked Ronnie Brown to help me and he kindly supplied the lyrics. Then, I asked my friend John McNairn if he'd like to be involved and he was happy to fly down to Heathrow and spend a couple of days in the studio. And so, *Passions Cry* was born. It was recorded in Studio House, Wraysbury, Berkshire, with the help of Stuart Tosh and Ian Bairnson. I'd found my writing hat again and it seemed to fit.

The album was signed to Brian Adams' label WCP and released on cassette and CD under the name 'Davie Paton' in 1991.

1990 and 1991. Richard Thompson and Labi Siffre

Another happy phone call came in asking if I was available to work with Richard Thomson. Richard was recording the music for a movie called *Sweet Talker*.

Dave Mattacks would feature on drums and I'd be sharing the bass-playing duties with Danny Thompson.

We recorded in Angel Studios, London. I asked myself how I had the courage to walk into that environment and have the confidence to play for these guys! I had great admiration for Richard, and Danny is a legend. In fact, Danny and I played on one of the tracks together, with him on upright bass and me on fretless.

A few days after the Richard Thompson session, I did another session for Labi Siffre. It was a nightmare. Rod Argent was producing and I found it odd that Labi sat at the back of this church-like control room, complete with pews and he didn't appear very friendly. I sat at the desk with the engineer and the song was played to me. Rod and Labi stayed seated at the back of this huge control room, chatting endlessly. I started working on the song, but four bars into it I heard a shout from the back of the room, 'you're late, you're playing behind the beat'. I'm thinking,' I don't play late; I'm always spot on with the kick drum'. We start again, and the shout comes out again 'you're late'. I couldn't believe what I was hearing. I said, 'why don't you come and sit here instead of sitting at the back of the room?' That did not go down well at all. The engineer eventually spoke up for me and told them 'David is correct', they seemed to accept that perhaps I wasn't late, but their remarks put me on edge and I didn't enjoy the music or the atmosphere.

But I had the pleasure of meeting Paul Jones on that session. He's another musician I respect and I had enjoyed listening to and watching him early on in my career when he sang with Manfred Mann. He arrived to play blues harp (or mouth organ). He opened his specially designed case that held his instruments, but I noticed there were twelve spaces and only eleven were occupied; one was missing. He asked what key the song was in, Labi said Bb and, low and behold, that was the one that was missing, so Rod arranged for a biker to bring a Hohner mouth organ from a London music store. Blues harp players, as a rule, play in what is described as 'second position.' If a tune is in the key of Bb, an Eb harmonica will be used. So, not surprisingly, it was an Eb harp that was missing.

I didn't hang around after I finished as I found the environment a little hostile. I'm sure Labi didn't like me or my bass playing. I met Rod

Argent at a Zombies gig in Edinburgh and I mentioned the session to him. He remembered the Labi Siffre session and was sympathetic to my rather embarrassing experience. Suffice to say my bass part didn't make the album.

1991. Fish and Back to Scotland

Life in England had been fun and it was necessary to be there because of the work I was doing in and around London. But now, after nine years in Berkshire, I was feeling very homesick. My daughter Sarah had decided she wanted to live in Edinburgh, so off she went and she initially moved in with my Mum in Morningside. My younger daughter Katy was now ten years old; she was a toddler when we first moved south and had no recollection of living in Scotland. She'd been educated in England and spoke with an English accent. When I told her we were thinking of moving to Scotland, she got very upset and shed many tears at the thought of moving away from her friends in sunny Berkshire. But it was the right time for us, so we set the wheels in motion.

I performed at the Edinburgh Festival with Rick Wakeman, with just the two of us doing his *Classical Connection* concerts. We played an excellent gig at the Playhouse Theatre. I met Sarah for lunch and she told me that moving back to Edinburgh was the best thing for her at that time of her life. She was working as an estate agent on Morningside Road and had made friends with the local Morningside crew. So I got in touch with my mates and enjoyed a couple of beers and the Edinburgh night life. The *Evening News* invited me along to an event and presented me with the award Musician of the Festival, which was probably organised by my friend John Gibson who was a well-known reporter at the paper.

Our house in England sold quickly and during the preparation for the move, I received a call from John Cavanagh. He was managing Fish and asked me if I'd be interested in joining his band. I found it interesting that I was being asked to join Fish as he lived just outside Edinburgh. It seemed like fate had stepped in, so I agreed to a meeting. I had to audition, which I found a bit odd as I had never had to audition since The Beachcombers. But all went well and I was asked to join.

Although I was happy to be in a recording and gigging outfit, I felt a little bit out of place with the setup. I was happy to be in a band with Ted McKenna on drums. Ted was a wonderful player. He was the original drummer with the Sensational Alex Harvey Band and worked with Rory Gallagher, The Greg Lake Band, Michael Schenker and he toured with Ian

Gillan, but Fish wasn't happy with him. Things eventually came to a head and Ted left the band. Sadly Ted McKenna passed away in 2019.

Auditions for drummers took place in Fish's own studio The Funny Farm, in Haddington, East Lothian. We rehearsed almost every day without any let-up. Fish wasn't happy with the drummers he auditioned and was getting a bit anxious about it. I had an evening off and went to hear some friends play in a pub in Newington and although I didn't know the drummer – Dave Stewart – I was very impressed with his playing and took note of his contact details. Next day I was at the farm and suggested him, but Fish was not so keen. He said he'd auditioned him a year or so ago and wasn't sure if he was right for the band. Dave was a good ten years younger than the other members and I think Fish would have preferred an older and more established drummer, but he agreed to the audition. Dave absolutely walked it. His attention to detail was admirable, as he had really pinned down the songs we rehearsed and impressed everyone.

When the tour with Fish began to be put together, I started to realise that this was not the kind of touring I was keen to do. Travelling in a tour bus was not my idea of fun. I'd been spoiled working with Elton and this different kind of touring life had no appeal to me. This was the kind of thing I had done with The Beachcombers and The Rollers, and that was limited to touring Scotland. The bus tours with Fish would cover much greater distances around Europe and we'd be out on the road for at least two months at a time. We drove to Holland, France, Latvia, Lithuania and Estonia. I couldn't wait to get back home and found myself counting the days and marking them off on my tour book. The band were fine, all good players and we made the best of the discomfort. The sleeping quarters were upstairs on the bus with a small lounge area at the back. Downstairs was the kitchen and TV/video lounge. After gigs, Dave Stewart, Foss Paterson, Robin Boult and myself would sit in the upstairs lounge listening to the likes of Earth, Wind and Fire while the others would sit downstairs drinking coffee, watching videos or talking to Fish.

Fish could sometimes act the star. To be fair, he was always aware of it and asked me to let him know if I ever thought he was being a bit precious. We arrived for a full rehearsal to find that the band would be performing behind a semi-transparent net curtain. I was elected to talk to Fish and tell him the band were unhappy about being separated from the audience. He was angry that we objected, and when I mentioned him asking me to tell him when I thought he was being a bit precious, he was having none of it. But the nets did come down eventually.

We were in Eastern Europe when a call came into the production office. It was the great Free and Bad Company singer Paul Rogers wanting to speak to me. He asked me if I'd be able to join him for a tour of the USA. As the Fish tour was coming to an end, I said yes. He said he'd get his manager to get the visa sorted and would be in touch in a couple of days. The call came back from his manager, and he explained that as I was in Eastern Europe at the time, it would be impossible to have the visa processed in time for the tour as my passport was needed. Of course, I was bitterly disappointed.

1993. The Pretenders and Chrissy Hynde

I'd been a big fan of The Pretenders since I heard their hit 'Brass in Pocket'. I always liked Chrissie Hynde, as she has a good, expressive voice and writes excellent songs. It was a pleasant surprise when I was invited to play bass on one track on the new Pretenders album. The track I would be working on was 'I'll Stand By You'. The recording took place in Sarm studios, London, so I flew down from Edinburgh and made my way to the studio.

Former Tears For Fears keyboardist Ian Stanley was producing and he greeted me when I arrived. As soon as I was set up, we started work on the song. For a bass overdub like this, it's normal for the musician to sit in the control room with the producer, as communication is a lot easier. I learned the track fairly quickly and the bass part was finished when Chrissy arrived. She was dressed in jeans and a jumper, with no makeup and was looking pretty relaxed. We all listened to the playback and she was delighted, so she asked me if I could play on a few other tracks, which was fine by me as I didn't fly back to Edinburgh till the next day. She pointed out four more songs that she'd like to hear me play on and as I was enjoying the music, it was great to play on those too. Chrissy said she'd return in a couple of hours, so I got my head down and played on the songs that she had marked out for me. On her return, she looked great – she was made-up and had changed into a short skirt and thigh-length boots. We chatted and I was treated to a few Bob Dylan impressions, which were hilarious. All was going well and I felt at ease with her. She has a great personality and I was fascinated by her recollections of some of the personalities she knew. When I meet well-known musicians, they tend not to hold back on their stories, as I guess they must do on chat shows. In a less formal setting, they just become musicians like me, and the addition of a famous face can make it all the more entertaining.

We listened to the songs and she was delighted and said she really liked my playing. While I was packing up in the studio, Ian Stanley came in and said that Chrissy was thrilled and would like me in her band; he asked me if I was interested. That was something I didn't expect to hear; I was a bit surprised and taken aback. Thinking on my feet about my commitment to Fish, I said to Ian I was sorry, but I couldn't do it. He walked back to the control room and after a few minutes, I heard Chrissy yelling at him. She sounded very angry and upset. I wondered if it was because of me, but I didn't hang about to find out. When the album was released, I noticed I was only featured on one track, 'I'll Stand By You'. It was a snap decision and If I'd been persuaded a bit more or if I'd been given time to think it over, I might well have said yes. Once again, my loyalty to the guy I was playing bass for at the time clouded my judgement.

1995. Phil Cunningham

My friend Jon Turner owned Palladium Studios in Edinburgh. He has worked with some of Scotland's best artists, including Capercaillie, Phil Cunningham and Ally Bain, The River Detectives, The Cocteau Twins, Del Amitri and Runrig. I was recording with Jon when he mentioned Phil Cunningham and said he was in need of a bass player. Phil is involved with Scottish and Gaelic music and is a very accomplished multi-instrumentalist. He's a bit of a legend in Scotland and highly respected not only in music but also for his television and radio work. Jon arranged for me to meet Phil at the studio which was just a couple of miles from my house.

I thought this was going to be quite a formal meeting and maybe a play through some tunes together. Instead, we sat in the sunroom telling each other jokes for about an hour. I was in need of a good laugh and I certainly got it from Phil. He's such a naturally funny guy, but we eventually talked about working together. Phil had many projects on the go and I found myself travelling from Edinburgh to his house and studio in Beauly-Inverness on a regular basis. Phil also did a lot of TV work at that time, so we were very often involved in STV and BBC programs.

One New Year, I did a pre-record for the STV *Hogmanay Show* with Rab Noakes. I was then asked to do the live Hogmanay show for BBC Scotland with Phil, so I was on both channels for their Hogmanay shows. That must have been a first!

Working with so many Scottish artists got me thinking about *Passions Cry*. I called Brian Adams and asked him if I could license the songs from him as I'd like to re-release the album. He said he had plans for the songs and refused to even consider a license for me to use the recordings.

I spoke to Jon Turner about this. He suggested that I re-record the songs with him at his studio. He introduced me to Gus McDonald at KRL records in Glasgow, who was happy to put up the recording budget and release the album on his label. Jon and I started to make plans for the recordings to get started. I could now bring in some excellent musicians to help create the Scottish flavour I needed for the songs.

I managed to get Phil Cunningham to play the accordion for me, James Mackintosh on percussion, Malcolm Stitt on bagpipes and whistles, plus John McNairn and my friends Robin Boult and Kevin Wilkinson. Thanks to Jon's expertise, the album sounds great. But I now had the recording bug and decided to invest in some pro-quality equipment for myself.

1995. Back with Elton

Davey Johnstone called me out of the blue. I really didn't expect this call but he explained the current bass player with Elton (Bob Birch) had been involved in a traffic accident and would need a few months to recuperate. They needed someone for an upcoming tour of USA and South America. This offer arrived at the right time for me as I felt like I was in a bit of a rut. Within two weeks, I was on my way to New York to start rehearsals for the tour, although one small problem was that I didn't have my working visa and this would need to be organised before the start of the gigs. It was arranged that I would fly from New York to Canada as I had to be out of the USA to apply for the visa. I had an overnight stay in Toronto then I was back in New York the next day.

I was sitting in the dressing room on my own when Elton arrived for the first rehearsal. I heard him asking where I was, and he came into the room and gave me a big hug and thanked me for helping out. I told him I was delighted and happy to be back, even though it was just a temporary position. I'd done my homework and was well up to date with all the songs that would be played in the set.

Things had changed from the time I was with the band between 1985 and 1988. There were no more parties and no meetings in the bar after the gig. It had become very civilised and quiet for a rock and roll tour, far removed from my earlier days with the band. It had been well documented that Elton had cleaned up his act and was living a healthy lifestyle, but so was the entourage. Everyone seemed to be walking about with a bottle of water in their hands, going to the gym and being careful with what they ate and drank. As a result, I didn't see anyone during the day and found myself visiting shopping malls alone. The hotels were excellent and there was usually a limousine on hand to take me to the mall. I was reminded on a few occasions that the arrangement was only there temporarily and that Bob was the bass player. I quickly got the message and I wasn't after Bob's job and I was just happy to be there. I wasn't there hoping I'd be asked back; I was helping out and I was prepared to be finishing up after we played South America. A get-well-soon card was being signed by everyone for Bob and they politely asked me to sign it. I wished him a speedy recovery and my good wishes were sincere.

The tour kicked off for me in New York at Madison Square Gardens. I loved the gigs – who wouldn't – being on stage was the best time and I felt at home playing and interacting with everyone. We had ten days in New York and six glorious gigs at MSG.

I'll give you an idea of how things were when the last note of the gig was played. We took our bows and as we walked down the steps backstage, each member of the band was handed a white hooded robe and a towel. We were ushered onto a waiting bus to be whisked back to the hotel. Instructions were given to leave our stage clothes and shoes outside our hotel room door. The clothes would be collected, taken to the dry cleaners and would be in the dressing room at the next gig. We'd be performing in front of 20,000 people and within no time at all, I was in a hotel room, in silence but still buzzing after a really fantastic show and thinking, 'What the fuck?' There was no way I was going to sleep after that excitement.

After the first gig, I made my way down to the bar and was delighted to hear Davey Johnstone talking to the barman. He was sitting at the bar and had champagne in a bucket beside him and was smoking a rollup. I wasn't sure if he would be pleased to see me, but he invited me to sit with him. We chatted, swapping stories and recollections of Edinburgh. There's nothing false about Davey; he's down to earth, friendly, good company and has some amazing recollections.

After a while, we left the hotel bar and made our way to our rooms. When we exited the elevator, I saw a guy ahead of us. As we got closer, I realised it was famed singer-songwriter, Jackson Browne. He was fumbling with his room key. As we approached, he said hello to Davey. I was delighted they knew each other and Davey introduced me as Elton's bass player, which made me smile. It was a quick meeting, but it was still a thrill to meet someone whose music means a lot to me.

Unfortunately, the crew would either be in another hotel or on the road to the next gig, so there wasn't much socialising with them, although I remember one occasion when the band were invited by the crew to a Halloween party in upstate New York. Mary had flown out for a few days and both of us were happy to accept the invitation; Davey Johnstone also made it. We had a really happy day relaxing and hanging out with the guys.

After the New York concerts, we flew to Buenos Aires, Argentina. This was my first visit to South America, and I thought Buenos Aires was stunning – I found myself comparing it to the grandeur of Paris. In a survey by *Travel and Leisure Magazine*, visitors voted Buenos Aires the second most desirable city to visit after Florence in Italy.

John Jorgenson called me and invited me to an exclusive nightclub where we could have a drink and be entertained with some proper Tango dancing. We had an excellent night out and got a real flavour of the Buenos Aires nightlife. But Colombia was a totally different experience. Bogota is rated the 7th most dangerous city in the world. We stayed for just two nights and were told not to leave the hotel.

The last gig of the tour was the VH1 awards on December 3 1995. Tina Turner joined us on stage for 'The Bitch is Back'. We had a rehearsal with her but she knew her part really well and we only needed to run through the song a couple of times. Elton sang the first verse and Tina appeared strutting her stuff (like only Tina can) across the stage towards Elton. That was another surreal experience for me.

Also on the bill was Prince. I'm often star-struck and seeing Prince just knocked me out. There was a large area backstage and I was watching what was going on when Prince walked by me as he made his way onto the stage. He was on his own and was wearing an amazing sparkly red suit with bell-bottom trousers and high heel boots. The cuffs of his shirt were frilly and he was adjusting them as he walked past me, but I was just delighted I'd managed to get so close to him!

Another artist on the bill was Chrissy Hynde with The Pretenders. I'd been speaking with Elton in the dressing room when he said, 'Oh, I see the Pretenders are here, I think I'll go and say hello to Chrissy'. I said to him I played on her latest album. 'I'll Stand By You' had been released in 1994 and was a massive hit for her. Elton said, 'well, let's both go and say hello to her'. We made our way to her dressing room and Elton knocked on the door. The door was opened by a really big, smartly dressed guy – a personal bodyguard, no doubt. He didn't speak, just looked at us. Elton said, 'we've come to say hello to Chrissy'. The big guy said, 'hold on'. The door closed and we looked at each other. Elton was smiling. The door opened again and the big guy said, 'Chrissy has a headache', and with that he seemed to slam the door shut. Elton looked at me again and brought his hand up to his face; we were both doubled over with laughter at the rebuff.

But that was it. The tour ended, and I made my way back to Edinburgh.

1996 onwards. Recording Scottish musicians

I rented a room for writing and recording in Hart Street Studios, Forth Street, Edinburgh. The studio had originally been owned by The Corries. As a reminder, my old art teacher Roy Williamson was one half of the Corries who wrote 'Flower of Scotland'. Hart Street Studios was now in the hands of Roy Ashby, a very likeable character who became a good friend while I worked there. I was lucky enough to work with the legendary folk singer Dick Gaughan on his *Redwood Cathedral* album, also recorded in Hart Street. Dick is a Scottish musician, singer and songwriter, particularly of folk and social protest songs and is regarded as one of Scotland's leading singer-songwriters. I also recorded there with another renowned folk singer Archie Fisher. He is a lovely, gentle guy and I enjoyed working on his album, which began life in the mid-90s. I recorded with him in 2003, but it took him until 2008 to complete and release *Windward Away*.

Hart Street eventually closed and I moved my studio into my garage and started recording local artists. This was highly successful and enjoyable too. During this time, I worked with many Scottish artists, including Dougie McLean, Fiona Kennedy, Donnie Munro, Capercaillie, McAllias and Holly Thomas, Andy M. Stewart, Blair Douglas and many more. My friends Nobby Clark and Kenny Herbert were also regular visitors to my home studio.

The music and the fun times continued with Phil Cunningham. We travelled to New York to perform at the annual Tartan Day Parade, showcasing pipers and drummers who honour the contribution Scots have made to the USA. It was 2002, and only a few months after the 9/11 attack on the World Trade Center in 2001. My daughter Sarah was living in New York at that time, and we had some time together before I flew back to the UK.

I was still working with Donnie and Phil Cunningham when I started thinking about a move to Spain.

Spain

2003. The move to Spain

By the time the new millennium dawned, I was beginning to move on in life and I was working with established artists a lot less. I always say, 'nothing lasts forever' and I accept what comes my way. Que sera sera. In 2003 I was 54 years old and thinking of giving up on travelling the world. I was also aware of time passing, so a move to a more agreeable climate was becoming very appealing. There is a saying that I was very conscious of at that time, which was 'Live a life of going to do, die with nothing done'.

The weather in Edinburgh was getting me down. I became very aware of it. 2003 must have been a particularly bad year in Scotland. We had a lovely garden, but I found myself looking out of the rain-spattered patio door windows and watching the wild weather play havoc with the shrubs and vegetable patch. Tilly (our Westie) was just a pup then, and we were trying to house-train her. It was a nightmare.

When my sister-in-law invited us to join them on a holiday to Spain, we were happy to do so. They had some kind of timeshare deal and had landed a two-bedroom apartment in a place called Dénia on the Costa Blanca. We didn't know what to expect and just thought we'd have a relaxing time in a beautiful area with nice weather.

The flight to Alicante is around 3 hours from Edinburgh. It's a nice short flight, and there's a massive difference in climate. We travelled by car from the airport to Dénia, which is about a 40-minute drive north of Alicante. The drive from the airport is stunning and the coastline of the Costa Blanca is wonderfully dynamic. Dénia is home to a large Moorish castle on a rocky crag overlooking the city. It was built in the 11th and 12th centuries and offers views around the sea, the city and the surrounding area. Located in the castle are the Palau del Governador and its museum. Mary and I loved the place as soon as we entered this lovely town. It is also a port and a popular gateway to the Balearic Islands.

We visited the indoor market and were delighted to hear a band playing. We sat down at an indoor café and watched some locals dancing and singing along to the band. It really was a great atmosphere. It seemed to me that Dénia was putting on a show for us, welcoming and seducing us with all these temptations. When we walked back out into the sunshine, I said to Mary, 'I could live here', and she agreed. We discussed it while we walked back to the apartment and thought we could give it a try for two or three years. I realized that we could do this quite easily. There was nothing stopping us from doing it; no obstacles. The idea of living in Spain for a couple of years began to sound very feasible and very tempting and as we walked by an estate agent, we stopped and looked at the properties for sale. After looking for a good ten minutes, we walked into the agent's office. Marcos was the owner and he didn't speak English very well. He was German, so it was German or Spanish, and we settled on a kind of Spanglish. Somehow, we managed to arrange a meeting with him for the next morning, when he would take us to look at three properties.

We didn't like either of the first two places, but the third was lovely. The garden had a dozen orange trees, lemon trees, oleander and bougainvillaea. The kitchen would need extending, but we could visualize the improvements we needed to make. Getting paperwork done in Spanglish is not easy, but lucky for us, Marcos was on the level and it went smoothly. We did have trouble with our house sale, but it did go through eventually.

The interesting part about the Spanish story is that Ian and Leila Bairnson moved to Javia, which is only about five or six kilometres from where we were in Dénia. Jon Turner moved to Dénia and is still there to this day, where he is married to Maria, a lovely Spanish girl. Stuart Tosh now lives not far from Alicante to the south. Taking into account that Billy Lyall was a fluent Spanish speaker, it seems that we find a powerful Spanish connection with the members of Pilot.

For the first few months, I was happy spending a lot of time enjoying the new lifestyle and putting music on the back burner. But after a while, I started to set up a studio in the garage and was soon spending time recording ideas.

Nobby came over to record and that was fun having someone else in the studio to work with. Shortly after that, Kenny Herbert, Nobby and Rab Howat came over for a week and we started recording an album for Kenny and Rab. The songs were really good and we were all being very creative and enjoyed the company and sunshine. They brought with them a DVD of a new show called *Still Game*, a hilarious Scottish TV comedy that had us falling about laughing but also succeeded in making us feel homesick. It was really great having the guys there and they had their own self-contained apartment upstairs. Aye, there was a swimming pool and a lovely garden. With the town a short walk away, it was just like being on holiday and having the luxury of recording at a leisurely pace.

We were very happy there. Jon would pop round and have a swim, and we could arrange evening meals with Ian and Leila or Jon and enjoy the climate; that made a big difference to our lives.

A Japanese band made contact with me – they went by the name of Beagle Hat. My main contact with them was Hisa Tanaka. He asked if I would sing a song on their album. I agreed and they sent the files to me and asked me to translate the lyric for them. The song was entitled 'Casgabarl', which is the name of the town in which Hisa was raised. It tells the story of Hisa's memories of growing up, his family and the poverty they endured. There is a section of the song that deals with Japanese childhood and the story of The Ghost. This part of the story was probably from a children's book. Here's a sample of the lyric:

Who's not sleeping who's not sleeping
you, you, or you, which one
The Ghost is coming to get the children
with an empty stomach too.
Don't you know I'm happy, happy,
he can eat up many, very many children.
Let's get this one,
I'll have him for my dinner tonight.

That's a scary wee section of the song, but I'm sure all the kids were sound asleep by 9 pm.

The recording went very well and I was comfortable translating and singing the song. Beagle Hat were delighted. They wanted to hear me sing more, so they asked me to add vocals to all the songs on the album. Eventually, Hisa arranged to come and visit me in Dénia. He was accompanied by a crazy friend who became very popular with the locals when he joined in with them during the running of the bulls through the town of Dénia and down to the harbour. This was the start of a long friendship and collaboration with Hisa and Beagle Hat.

By 2006, The Beagle Hat album was ready for production, but they still needed a title for it. Hisa asked me if I had any ideas, and I told him I'd think about it. Meanwhile, I sent him a 'See You, Jimmy' hat for his son as I knew he had a birthday coming up. I told him it was a magical hat, and that every time he put it on, it would make people very happy. He loved the hat and told me we had the title for the album – *Magical Hat*.

Right: Onstage in Dundee. (*Marc Marnie*)

Below: Onstage in Germany. (*David Paton Collection*)

With Ian Bairnson in 2018. (*David Paton Collection*)

Promoting *The Magic Collection* in 2022. (*David Paton Collection*)

Coming Home

2005 and 2006. A trip to Edinburgh and a permanent return to Scotland

I would return from Spain to Scotland each Hogmanay to take part in the BBC Hogmanay show with Phil Cunningham. Tilly (our Westie) had her own passport with a photo inside, which was really cute. We always drove from Dénia to Edinburgh because of Tilly and because it was a nice adventure and we enjoyed it. We really liked driving through France and then arriving at a hotel on the way. There were some memorable evening meals sitting outside in a courtyard or beautiful garden, watching the sunset while sipping the French wine and enjoying the cuisine. Tilly was always made welcome at the hotels and dogs were allowed in the restaurants, although, of course, we were eating alfresco most of the time.

It would take us around three days to drive from Dénia to Edinburgh, a total of 1600 miles. There was never any rush and I'd drive a maximum of eight hours in a day.

It was while I was on one of these return visits that I met up with my friend Nobby Clark and we took a walk up the High Street. We noticed a sign at the entrance to a stairway saying, 'Clairvoyant readings, please come in'. We decided it might be interesting, so we climbed the stairs. There were about eight clairvoyants in the room, and they were all busy when we walked in, so we sat together on a bench and waited for someone to approach us. As we sat together, I said to Nobby, 'don't tell them anything about yourself – let them do the talking'. A girl became available and came over to us. I told Nobby to go first but whispered, 'remember, don't tell her anything'. He walked with the girl to the far end of the room and they both sat down. Immediately I could see that Nobby was talking as she listened. I was thinking, what on earth is he telling her? Within a few minutes, a guy walked over to me and asked if a wanted a reading. I said 'yes' and followed him to a table and chairs. We sat down. He explained everything he was going to say and do in his distinctive Welsh accent. He said he'd record everything on cassette, and I could take it away with me after the reading. The first thing he said was, 'you're from Edinburgh, but you don't live here and you will return soon'. He then asked if I had high blood pressure, I said yes, but that it was controlled with medication. He said I should be careful about it, he spoke a bit about the blood pressure and let me know I should have it checked. I think he could sense a problem. He spoke to me for about 20 minutes. I could relate to everything he said, but the high blood pressure discussion concerned me.

We were staying with Mary's sister and her husband Ian, so on the way back to their house, I dropped into Boots The Chemist and bought a blood pressure monitor. After dinner, we sat in the lounge. I got the monitor out and took a reading, which was close to normal. Rose and Ian followed and their readings were also normal. I strapped the BP monitor to Mary's arm, expecting it to be normal also. The reading registered really high – alarmingly high. It was a Sunday evening, and we were heading back to Dénia in the morning. I persuaded Mary to take one of my BP tablets. I monitored her on the journey back and her blood pressure remained high but not as alarmingly so. Before heading back to Spain, we managed to get an appointment at our old doctor's surgery. After taking her blood pressure, he recommended that he book an appointment with the cardiology department in Edinburgh. He gave Mary a prescription and told her she'd receive a phone call with a date for the appointment, so she flew back to Edinburgh, where she was given the all-clear. Her blood pressure returned to normal, but I'm very glad the clairvoyant mentioned it.

Yes, I do believe there is something in clairvoyance and I'm very happy I had that reading. In fact, when we did move back to Edinburgh, I saw my Welsh clairvoyant again on a TV program about spiritualism.

Life in Spain was good, it was a slow pace and that's what we wanted when we made the move. We loved the town of Dénia and that leisurely way of life. Many happy days were spent walking through the town and visiting other parts of the surrounding area. Marques de Campo, the main Street in Dénia, is really excellent and full of cafes, restaurants and exclusive boutiques and shops. The only problem was that it was like being on an extended holiday. I soon began to miss the life we had in Edinburgh. We talked about it and Mary felt the same. We missed our daughters Sarah and Katy, we missed other family members and friends and we'd gone well beyond the two years we had planned on staying in Spain.

In 2006 we moved back to Scotland. We drove from Dénia to Edinburgh, but this time we didn't book hotels; we just took our chances of finding somewhere nice. It was a lovely drive up through Spain and we stopped in Southern France for an overnight stay. We then drove through France to Calais and stayed overnight in a hotel near the ferry port. The drive through England was long, dreary and tiresome. We had heavy traffic and thunderstorms with heavy rain all the way up to Carlisle.

We were about 40 miles from Edinburgh when Tilly started getting excited; she was agitated and sniffing frantically at the air vents. I honestly believe she knew where she was and was happy about being back in Scotland. When we reached Edinburgh, my phone rang. It was a keyboard player I'd worked with on a few local gigs, Kenny Hutchison. I liked his playing; he's a nice, friendly guy and taught general music studies at Loretto school in Musselburgh, just outside Edinburgh. He knew I'd been living in Spain and asked if I was still living there. I told him we'd just returned to Edinburgh that very day. Kenny went on to explain about a band he was putting together to perform at a new club opening soon in Queens Street, Edinburgh. The club would be known as The Jamhouse and Kenny explained that Jools Holland, the British TV presenter and musician, had an involvement with it. He asked if I'd be interested in playing bass in the band. Initially, my response was no, but he was quite insistent and asked me if I'd at least think it over. I said I would.

I was now 57 years old. I'd achieved a lot more in my career than I ever imagined. But to play in a resident band again after the heights I'd reached was making me think twice and I wasn't going to rush into a decision. I remembered the time I was doing a charity gig with some local musicians and a Radio Forth DJ who was also working at the gig said to me, 'Oh how the mighty have fallen'. Ouch! That hurt. But I love playing and I've never been selfish or egotistical about what I do. I'm a musician and music is my life. I'm well aware that nothing lasts forever and I'm happy making music, full stop. It wasn't for money; it was for the pure joy of it, and if some folk thought I'd taken a tumble, then so be it. I had been offered tours as Pilot, but I always turned them down.

But in fact, I tried one gig where it was Pilot and Liverpool Express on the same bill. Billy Livesley (of LE) came to me with his set list in his hand and asked me what songs we were playing. He wanted to make sure that we were not playing any of the songs that they would be playing. I told him that all our songs would be original Pilot songs. He was very surprised and said to me 'that's brave of you'. That threw me a bit. Liverpool Express were playing songs that any covers band would play. It was a terrible gig for me and I told the agent I didn't want to do any more chicken-in-a-basket performances like that as Pilot. We didn't play covers.

It was going to be a yes or no to Kenny's offer of playing at the Jamhouse, but I had nothing else in the pipeline, and I could be missing a great opportunity to gig every Friday and Saturday and have a lot of fun doing it. My daughters (Sarah and Katy) were at the house the following Sunday.

They told me that there was a big buzz going around the city about the Jamhouse and that I should definitely say yes to the offer. I called Kenny back the next day and told him I'd be happy to accept.

As it turned out, I found myself really enjoying being in this band and I looked forward to the gigs. The Flavours – the band I was in – were playing to 1000 people a night, and that's a lot more than the 350 that Rick Wakeman or Donnie Munro played to. I was in a covers band, but an excellent one, in which no one was the leader. We were a proper band playing a great selection of music and doing it really well. Not only that, but the pay was also better than I'd get with some of the established artists I'd worked with. After being there for five years, I remember Kenny saying to me 'do you realise that we have earned half a million in five years playing here'. I worked it out, and he was right. Some bands sign a five-year record deal and receive a half million advance, but the difference was that what we received wasn't an advance, and we didn't have to pay it back. We played at the Jamhouse for ten years and earned a million between us in that time. But as I said, it wasn't about the money, the best part and most important for me was that we made great music, and we had a ball doing it.

My ding-a-ling

In 2006, while we were still living in Spain, I noticed I was passing blood in my urine. It only happened once, but I got a fright as it seemed like a lot of blood. When we moved back to Edinburgh, the same thing happened again. It was a Sunday afternoon and Sarah and Katy were with us. I didn't want to say anything at that time. The next day I made an appointment with my doctor. He asked for a sample and although it looked clear, he said there was blood in it. He made a hospital appointment for me. I arrived at the day bed centre and was asked to strip and put on a blue gown. I was called and followed the nurse to a room with a trolley bed and asked to lie down. There were three nurses and a Dr Mackay, also female. She explained the procedure, which involved a camera being passed into my urethra and then into my bladder!

> Dr Mackay: OK, David, just place yourself on the bed and lie back; I'll be as quick as I can.

Woosh! Up with the gown and everything on view for all to see.

> Dr Mackay: I just need to rub this anaesthetic on the tip of your penis.

It wasn't too bad and I made a big effort to relax. The camera went in, and she had a look, and after five minutes at the most she was done. She said I had two cysts in my bladder, and that they had to be removed quickly. Within a week, I was in hospital having an operation. The procedure requires a general anaesthetic, but all went well and I was out of the hospital the same day.

I still attend the hospital every year for a check. The last time I was in, I went through the usual procedure of removing all my clothes and putting on the blue hospital gown that is open at the back and ties at the neck. I did all that, then sat in the waiting room waiting to be called.

I heard a voice say:' David Paton'? It was Nurse Andrena, and I'd seen her at the Jamhouse dancing at the front of the stage. She was standing smiling at me as if she knew what I'd been reading. I replaced the magazine on the table and we walked along to the theatre. I was greeted by three nurses and Dr Mackay. Dr Mackay had some questions for me, so I sat with her for a few minutes before starting the procedure.

The nurses do their best to put you at ease and they were asking me questions.

Nurse: Do you have the day off then, David?
Me: I'm self-employed and work from home.
Nurse: Oh, what do you do?
Me: I have a recording studio.
Nurse: Had anyone famous in your studio?
Me: I record mainly local musicians. Nobby Clark is a good pal; he uses my studio.
Nurse: Oh yes, he sang with The Bay City Rollers. I met Les McEwan once, and had my photo taken with him.
Me: Oh, that's nice. I met him too, we met on a TV show. Les was there with The Bay City Rollers.
Nurse: Oh! Were you in a band?

At that point, Dr Mackay interrupted and said, 'OK David, can you lie on the bed now'. I lay back and Woosh! Up with the hospital gown as I had the first time and Dr Mackay said (once again) ' I'm just going to rub this gel around the tip of your penis to numb it a little'. In went the camera again, which is attached to a long tube with a small lens on the end, a bit like a small telescope, I suppose.

Nurse: So, were you in a band?
Me: Yes, I was in a band called Pilot.

By this time, I had all of them looking at me.

Nurses: Oh, What songs did you perform? Would we know any of them?
Me: I wrote a song called 'Magic' and another called 'January'.

I didn't expect these youngsters to know the songs.

Nurses: Is that the song that goes 'Oh ho ho it's Magic?'
Me: Yes.
Dr Mackay (with a big smile): Oh really! Could you sing it for us now?
Me: Aye, that'll be right.
Dr Mackay: nearly done.

I saw some movement behind me and slightly to the right. I glanced round and saw another two nurses at the doorway looking at me, saying, 'that's him there'. Ha ha, word travels fast. I really couldn't have made that up and I did see the funny side of it even if they didn't. Me, lying there, exposed for all to see and they wanted me to sing 'Oh ho ho it's Magic'. I did see Andrena at the Jamhouse sometimes. One time I arrived at the hospital and she was on a day off. The nurses told me it was her birthday at the weekend and she'd be at the Jamhouse. I saw her in the crowd and waved at her. I approached the microphone and wished her a very happy birthday.

But I wish we had learned to play Chuck Berry's 'My ding-a-ling'...

2007. The Fellow Man album and the Countdown Spectacular tour

I started to write my album *Fellow Man* in early 2007. I didn't have the title song at that time, so the album was just a collection of new songs as the writing continued.

In 2007 I was also invited to Australia to take part in the *Countdown Spectacular*. For those who don't know, Countdown was the Australian equivalent of the UK's *Top of the Pops*. The *Countdown Spectacular* tour was a star-studded 1970s bill featuring Rick Springfield, Martha Davis of The Motels, Doug Fieger Of The Knack, Katrina Leskanich, formerly of

Katrina & The Waves, Plastic Bertrand, Les McKeown, formerly of The Bay City Rollers, Richard Gower of Racey, Robin Scott alias 'M', Samantha Fox, Graham Bonnet… and David Paton of Pilot. Birtles Shorrock Goble (founding members of Little River Band), Richard Clapton, Rockin' Doc Neeson's the Angels, Kate Ceberano (I'm Talking), Supernaut (reforming specially), The Radiators, Sharon O'Neill, John Schumann of Redgum, Dave Mason of The Reels, Ignatius Jones of Jimmy & The Boys and Paul Gray of Wa Wa Nee all took part

I was given a business-class flight to Sydney as part of the deal. My flight arrived early in the morning and I was met by a couple of crew members. They'd booked me a room in a hotel at the airport so that I could have a couple of hours sleep before the run-through with the house band. I did sleep for a couple of hours, had a shower and a bite to eat before being whisked off to meet the band and crew. Paul Gray from the band Wa Wa Nee was the musical director and we got straight into the chord structure of the songs before the rest of the band arrived. All went well. I was delighted with the band and their interpretation of the pieces and I only had to sing 'Magic' and 'January', so it was a breeze.

While in Sydney, I met with an old friend Andrew Hogarth. Andrew has a great interest in the indigenous people of Australia and USA. He wanted to introduce me to a well-known Aboriginal named Uncle Max. Andrew took me to a church where Uncle Max was performing a ceremony. I took my seat in one of the pews and Uncle Max appeared in traditional dress and his body was painted, it was a really impressive sight and a first for me to see an Aborigine in the flesh. He moved slowly down the aisle, fanning smoke from a basket with smoldering emu bush he was carrying. This is a tradition to acknowledge ancestors, ward off evil spirits, and heal and cleanse the place and the participants. Scientists have even proved the medicinal properties of burning emu bush.

Uncle Max was accompanied by a younger relative, and after the ceremony, Andrew introduced me. He said 'This is David Paton, he has travelled from Scotland'. Max said, 'You've come a long way'. I was really thrilled to be introduced to Uncle Max and he fired my imagination and inspired me. When I got back to the hotel, I started writing the words to a song with the working title of 'You've Come A Long way'. These are the words to the finished song:

Fellow man, what do you wanna be
Oh you've come a long way,

from the bottom of the sea
Oh you've come a long way,
that's what frightens me

There you go, running wild and free
Oh you've come a long way
From the wild to the city
Oh you've come a long way
How long are you gonna stay

We might as well enjoy it all
Cause nothing stays the same
And if we just destroy it all
There's no-one else to blame
While the sun gives us the light
And the moon will rise again
Let's keep alive the message
Let peace and love remain

Mother earth, what are you gonna do
Oh you've come a long way
From the wild to the city
Oh you've come a long way
How long are you gonna stay

I eventually renamed the song and album *Fellow Man*. Meeting my 'fellow man' from Australia made me realize that Uncle Max really is just that. We may be many miles apart, not only in distance but also in culture. He inspired me and filled me with awe. Looking into those wise eyes, I saw a 'human' in the true sense of the word.

This is the tour itinerary:

Sat 18 Aug 2007. Newcastle. Entertainment Centre,
Tue 21 Aug 2007. Brisbane. Entertainment Centre
Fri 24 Aug 2007. Sydney. Acer Arena
Tue 28 Aug 2007. Hobart. Derwebt Entertainment Center
Thur 30 Aug 2007. Melbourne. Rod Laver Arena
Sun 02 Sept 2007. Adelaide. Entertainment Centre
Wed 05 Sept 2007. Perth. Burswood Dome.

I really enjoyed that tour. I loved standing up in front of an audience who sang the words to my songs along with me. I enjoyed meeting and being with the other artists, becoming friends and sometimes hanging out together.

I had a lovely evening meal with Doug Fieger from The Knack, famous for the song 'My Sharona'. We realised that we had a lot in common. I had a fascinating talk with Doc Neeson of The Angels about songwriting and lyrics in particular. I spent many happy hours with John Paul Young ('Love Is In The Air'), who was presenting the show. He told me about his early life in Glasgow and how he came to be in Australia. I mention these three people because I really enjoyed being with them. I know I could have had a great friendship with them just because we clicked. Sadly, Doug and Doc Neeson are no longer with us. I've come to accept that as part of life, it has to end sometime, and for some, it comes far too early.

I also met Les McKeown of The Bay City Rollers for the first time. We met at the hotel in Newcastle, New South Wales. I was sitting outside enjoying the sun when Les walked over to me. He said, 'Hey, we meet at last'. He sat beside me and we spoke for a while. We didn't get around to the subject of Tam Paton or The Rollers, but I'm sure if we'd had more time together, we could have spoken for hours. He was friendly, talkative and easygoing. I liked Les, although I could see he had a fondness for alcohol that was way beyond my level of tolerance. We made friends and I began to understand him. Les, Sam Fox, her partner and I had lunch together and there was quite a lot of alcohol consumed. Conidering we had a show that evening, I had to leave them to it – lightweight!

You sometimes hear stories about well-known pop stars, which can influence your thoughts on what kind of person he or she is. A lot of the time, it's just nonsense and I found that Les and I had a lot in common, and we really did get on well together.

December 2008. Pins and needles

For a few months, I'd been a little concerned about my health. I like biking and had noticed a little sharp pain in my chest when I really pushed myself. It was enough for me to make an appointment with the doctor for a check.

In early December, I was getting ready for my gig at the Jamhouse. I had my shower and found that I still felt a bit too hot when I dressed and headed off for the gig. As I walked along Queen Street, I felt strange, a slight feeling of anxiety in my chest; it felt uncomfortable. When I walked into the dressing room, I spoke to Jim McDermott and asked him if I looked alright. He said I looked great, so I felt reassured. The strange feeling disappeared and I forgot about it. I had my ECG and blood test with the doctor and made an appointment for Friday, the 19th, to find out the results. I arrived at the doctor's surgery at 8.40 am and I was told that my ECG was fine; a good strong heartbeat with no apparent problems. My blood pressure was high but not extreme and my cholesterol test was also high, 6.9, but again, not extreme. My doctor informed me that if I had another anxiety attack, I should have a 24-hour monitor.

I left the surgery and went straight to work in the studio with a singer by the name of Jamie McBride. We finished in the studio at around 1.30 pm and I headed off to the Gyle shopping centre to get a couple of presents for Mary. While I was shopping, I started to feel the anxiety attack come over me again, it was stronger than before and I needed to sit down. I went for a cuppa and realised something serious was happening to me. Mary called my mobile for a chat and I answered her but was unable to concentrate on what she was saying to me. She said 'you're not listening to me, are you?' I told her I felt unwell. She told me to call an ambulance, but I said I'd get in my car and drive home and she said she'd meet me there. I was feeling bad now and I'd also forgotten where I'd parked my car. The weather was dreadful – high wind and rain battered the area as I staggered about the car park, occasionally stopping to catch my breath. At last, I found my car and slumped into the driver's seat, relieved to be sitting down again. After a few minutes, I started the engine and drove through the start of the Friday rush hour traffic to my house. The climb up the stairs sapped my strength and I just fell into bed with Tilly, our dog, giving me strange looks. Her ears were back and I remember thinking that she knew something was wrong with me. Within a few minutes, I heard Mary come in and she rushed upstairs. She took one look at me and said, 'Right, you have two choices, get in the car with me now, or I call an ambulance'. I told her I just needed to lie in bed and I'd be fine, but no, she was having none of it. 'Get your shoes on – you're coming to the hospital with me NOW!' I agreed reluctantly. Remembering about my gig that night, I called Kenny Hutchison and told him I was unwell. He told me not to worry and wished me well.

On arrival at the hospital, I explained my problem and was given a wheelchair and taken into the accident and emergency department while Mary sat in the waiting area. The pain was bad now. I sat in the wheelchair and watched the activity around me. A&E at the Edinburgh

Royal Infirmary has a large oblong reception area in the middle and is surrounded by cubicles with curtains. All the cubicles were taken and there were a few people sitting in wheelchairs and lying on beds around the reception area. I asked one of the staff if he had something for my pain, and he told me they were preparing a cubicle for me – I'd be seen to shortly. Someone came along and I was wheeled into the cubicle and transferred onto a bed. Mary appeared at this point and sat on my right-hand side. A doctor appeared and introduced himself as Dr Boon. He asked me lots of questions about the pain, when it started, and how bad it felt. I was wired up to various monitors and he informed me that I was having a heart attack. Although I was a little shocked, I wasn't in a panic. He also said that they were going to inject a clot-buster drug into me to dissolve the clot in my heart. The nurse was working to get a cannula in my arm when I suddenly felt pins and needles in my fingers; they started to travel up my left arm, I turned to Mary and said, 'pins and needles', she asked if I was OK and I said 'No, I'm not right'. A grey mist started to descend over my eyes, and I remember thinking, 'if this is the end, it's pretty painless'. I blacked out.

What happened next was unknown to me at the time, but Mary said that I looked at her and my eyes just glazed over, they were open and looking at her, but she knew I wasn't there. She shouted to the nurse, 'he needs help'. The nurse looked at me and gasped. She rushed out and shouted for the crash team. Doctors and nurses came running while Mary rushed out of the cubicle shouting, 'help him, help him'. She told me that all the patients and staff were looking at her in horror. They worked on me for a while and when I came round, I heard Mary say 'I want to stay with him', but they wouldn't let her. I managed to say 'I'm alright now', but she didn't hear me. I didn't ask the doctors what happened and they didn't tell me, but I did have a large bruise on my side that I can't explain, though I don't want to jump to conclusions.

After 20 minutes or so, they let Mary back in beside me. She told me it had been the most frightening time of her life. She really thought I was gone. The clot buster was taking effect and the pain was easing in my chest. I started to feel good again and told Dr Boon. He informed me that the next 24 hours were critical to my recovery and that if I was going to have another attack, it would happen within that period. As they wheeled me to cardiac high dependency, I smiled at Mary and told her that I felt fine.

I did feel fine. I wanted to sit up and say, 'I'm going home now' – silly boy. Mary stayed with me until Dr Boon appeared again and said he wanted to scan my heart. He seemed pleased with the scan and said that the damage appeared minimal. There was a bit of numbing and he pointed it out to me; he also said that the numbing would heal, although I would have a scar after the operation I would undergo.

I fell asleep and was wakened during the night for ECG and blood tests. In the morning, when the lights came on, I saw two nurses sitting at their desks in front of me. It was quiet, apart from the noise from the fans cooling the monitors around my bed. The tea lady offered me a cuppa and I lay there trying to take in my situation. A cleaning lady appeared from a door in the far corner. She was wearing the most amazing red felt hat covered with mistletoe, holly and flashing coloured lights. She didn't look very happy, but the hat cheered me up. She was sweeping her way around the ward. When she got close to cleaning around my bed, I said to her, 'Nice hat' and she said, 'I could dae withoot wearing it today. I'm no in the mood fir it'. She disappeared behind me and emerged with a pair of headphones in her hand. With a big smile, she said, 'you're a lucky boy, I've got you a pair of headphones and they're the only ones on this ward, I'll let you put them on, but you must sing along with whatever you hear, can you sing?'

I had been admitted on a Friday night, they didn't perform operations at weekends, so I had to wait until Monday, December 22 2008. So, I had a weekend in hospital, in a ward with three other men. It was fine and I got on well with the other guys. We were all in the same boat and made the best of it.

I was wheeled into the operating theatre on the Monday morning and as I lay there, a nurse asked me to choose the music they would play throughout the day. She said, 'you can choose between pop, jazz or classical'. I thought classical would be relaxing, so asked for that. But on came 'The Ride Of The Valkyries'. It's a very stirring and lively piece and not quite what I expected. The surgeon who would be fitting my stent walked in and asked who chose the music, and they all said, 'Mr Paton'. He was spinning a coffee cup around his finger and said, 'OK, who's going to make me a nice cup of coffee?' He walked over to me and introduced himself as Doctor Flapan, then he asked me, 'so Mr Paton, what do you do for a living?' I thought, oh, here we go again. I said 'I'm a musician'.

Dr Flapan: 'A general musician or do you specialise?'
Me: I'm known for my bass playing and I've had a bit of success with my songwriting'.

Dr Flapan: 'Oh, have you written any songs that I might know?'
Me: I wrote a song called 'Magic'.

With that, he sang at the top of his voice, 'Oh, ho ho, it's magic', then the nurses joined him for 'never believe it's not so'. He then went on to tell me how much the song meant to him and how delighted he was to meet me. In fact, they all managed to recall happy memories associated with 'Magic'. With that, he attached a canula to my wrist and proceeded to insert a long tube which went into my wrist and travelled all the way to my heart. He then told me that I had a narrow artery and he could insert a stent into my heart and open the artery up, if I was OK with that. I said that I'd be happy for that procedure to go ahead. I watched the monitor as the voyager stent travelled to the narrowed artery and was placed perfectly. He stood back, looked at the monitor and said, 'Beautiful, now, where's my cup of coffee'.

As I was wheeled out, I thanked everyone as I cried like a baby, so grateful and overwhelmed that my life would continue for a while longer. Now I felt fine; I could do what I wanted as long as I felt comfortable. Bike rides and walkies with Tilly didn't have me breathless or in pain, although I must avoid hoovering, dishes and any general housework duties, of course!

The Jamhouse beckoned and I was back there on New Years' Eve 2008, giving it all I'd got. Recovery was quick and complete, so they told me. It was another reality check for me and life is sweeter than ever.

2011. Brian Wilson

I received a Facebook friend request from Probyn Gregory. I googled him and found out that he was a member of The Brian Wilson Band. After accepting the friend request, I messaged him to say that I'd seen the concert by the band in Edinburgh and really enjoyed it. He told me he was also in a band called The Wondermints and their speciality was 70s music – they even played Pilot songs in their set.

The Wondermints are a power pop band from Los Angeles, California, who released four albums between 1995 and 2002, plus a reissues album in 2009. The main line-up consisted of Darian Sahanaja (keyboards), Nick Walusko (also known as Nicky Wonder on guitar), and Mike D'Amico (percussion). The band members are also known for serving as part of the backing band for Brian Wilson since the late 1990s. Other contributors to The Wondermints have included Brian Kassan (bass), David Nolte (bass) and Probyn Gregory (various instruments and vocals).

Probyn informed me that Brian Wilson was booked for a concert at The Royal Concert Hall on September 11 2011, in Glasgow and would I like to attend? Of course, I took him up on the offer, as it was only a few weeks away. Glasgow is only a 45-minute drive from Edinburgh. I travelled through with Mary playing Beach Boys music on the journey to help set the mood.

A Brian Wilson concert is very special. The songs are masterpieces of composition and the musicianship first class. I consider 'God Only Knows' to be the work of a genius, and Brian certainly holds that status for me. It was a joy to attend the concert the second time around.

I had arranged to meet Probyn after the show and I was delighted to be introduced to other members of the band. They all said they were delighted to meet me and held my songwriting in high regard. Compliments from other accomplished musicians are special to me, and it's a great feeling knowing I'd written a song that was respected musically as well as commercially.

Probyn asked if we would like to go backstage and meet Brian in his dressing room. Wow, I didn't really expect that. Brian was alone and having a bowl of pasta when we walked into the room. Probyn introduced me as David Paton, the guy who wrote 'Magic'. Brian reacted positively to this; he put down his pasta shook my hand and said, 'You wrote that song? I love that song – it's a great song'. He started to sing the chorus, while I just stood there in disbelief. Brian Wilson was singing my song to me. He continued talking and said, 'What a great song, I wish I'd written that'. We sat together for a photograph and instead of looking at the camera he looked at me and said 'Never believe it's not so'. It meant so much to me that Brian knew my song so well. I was so overjoyed.

2012. Under the Sun

I always intended to write another album after *Fellow Man*, but knowing where to start was the problem. My friend Kenny Hutchison gave Mary and me the use of his house in France for a week. There was a lovely Yamaha electric piano in one of the outhouses and I would sometimes venture there and have a play. 'Under the Sun' just popped into my head from nowhere. I didn't have the words, but I had the melody and I kept playing it and making small improvements each time I ran it through. I had the first song for a new album and that set the pace and gave me the enthusiasm to continue writing. The lyrics started to take shape and I realised I was singing about a health scare. Whether we suffer from a cold or a heart attack, the sentiment of the song is the same:

I wanna make love,
I wanna have fun,
I wanna have freedom,
under the sun.

Essentially what I'm saying is that we want to have our health back. The album entitled *Under the Sun* was released in 2012

At the dentist

I had an early morning dental appointment with Dr Gruber. When I walked in and up to reception, the receptionist said, 'Good morning David'. She had never called me by my first name before. She looked at me and said, 'I saw your interview in *The Evening News* with John Gibson'. She went on to say that she had watched the TV show *The Wizards of Waverley Place* with her niece and that my song features in it. At that, another receptionist turned round and looked at me. I caught her eye and said to her that every time I came in and said 'David Paton for Dr Gruber, ' she would look up the appointments and then say, 'OK, David, that's magic, have a seat'. The first time she said it, I smiled at her, but she just turned away and got on with her work. I thought she only said it to me until I was in a queue one time and she was saying it to everyone. 'Right Mr Smith, that's magic. Have a seat'. She told me that she wasn't aware of saying it and it was probably just habit. We had a good laugh when the other receptionist told her that I had written the song 'Magic'.

I liked to practise the few words I knew in German with my dentist Herr Gruber. I'd walk into his surgery and say 'Wie gehts?' ('How are you?') He'd answer in German and I know he found my accent very amusing. I generally didn't understand his reply, but I had rehearsed what I'd say to him 'Alles ist gut, ich bin glucklich mit den Zahnen'. (Everything is fine, I'm happy with my teeth). That always set a happy mood and we'd laugh. I'm sure his assistant thought I was a fluent German speaker, which I'm certainly not.

On my way out of the dental practice, I walked by the reception; the receptionist said, 'I've been singing that song of yours all morning; it's driving me mad'.

2014. A Pilot Project

Ian Bairnson and his wife Layla were still living in Spain when they found out that Ian had a degenerative brain condition. As a result, they were flying back and forward from Spain to Edinburgh for Ian to attend The Anne Rowling Regenerative Neurology Clinic at Edinburgh University.

We would always get together in my studio when he visited the hospital. We'd play through Pilot songs and Alan Parsons Project songs. I recorded a backing track for 'What Goes Up', which was a song I sang with APP on the *Pyramid* album. When Ian added guitar to the track, I realised how close we were to the original recording. After all, I'd sung the song originally, I'd also played bass and acoustic guitar and Ian had played acoustic and lead guitar. With the advances in technology, my studio was now of a very high standard, so we started putting our *Pilot Project* album together. I'd construct a backing track and either send it to Ian or have him play in the studio when he visited.

We were both enjoying getting back into playing together and doing something worthwhile musically. Ian and Leila eventually moved back to the UK and bought a house just outside Edinburgh. This made things a bit easier for Ian to complete the guitar parts and also attend the neurology clinic. It makes a big difference when you can work face to face and progress was much quicker when we were together in the studio. I could almost feel that Eric was with us as the music came together. What started out as a bit of fun became much more as we realised that by releasing *A Pilot Project* it would be a fitting tribute to Eric Woolfson and his legacy. It was also the 40th anniversary of Pilot's debut album and within a few months, we had our project completed. It was released in 2014.

2016 to 2019. Albert Hammond

I was contacted by Irene Bodschwinna from the Hypertension agency in Hamburg. Irene was the agent for Donnie Munro when I toured Germany with him in 2001. She told me that Albert was ready to ditch his Spanish band because of several fallouts between him and the band. She said they were disrespectful to Albert and he wanted to make the change during a three-week break he was planning.

Keyboardist Foss Paterson and I met Albert with Irene at a gig he performed in Dunfermline. I thought the band were good and I enjoyed a lot of the songs he'd co-written for other artists. I didn't think his voice had much character, but he sang well enough and we met up with him backstage after the gig. He seemed OK, he was certainly driven, and he made it clear that he wanted to play to bigger audiences. It sounded to me like that might be difficult for him as he was pretty much only known for 'The Free Electric Band and 'It Never Rains in Southern California'.

They're both very fine songs and were the hits he'd had in the 70s as a solo artist. He'd get very upset when he noticed artists like Chris De Burgh playing to 5000 people when he was playing to just 1000. But his songs were excellent. For example, I loved playing the song he and John Bettis wrote for Whitney Houston, 'One Moment In Time', and 'The Air That I Breathe', written with Mike Hazelwood, not to mention 'I Don't Wanna Lose You' written with Graham Lyle and released by Tina Turner

He was described by the people who worked for him as a bit self-centred. It was noticeable, but a lot of artists are like that, some to a lesser extent than others. Perhaps it's one of the traits needed to be successful. I liked Albert, and I understood what he wanted to achieve, even though I thought he'd be a happier person if he enjoyed the level he had already achieved. There were a couple of things I became aware of that I found a bit petty. He would make sure my microphone was set back from the front of the stage, and he told the lighting director to keep the band in shadow. He would never introduce us on stage and he didn't want us known as The Albert Hammond Band. I was there to play bass and have fun, so I didn't mind his idiosyncrasies and to begin with, I really enjoyed every aspect of the tours set up by Irene and Christian at Hypertension.

So Foss and I agreed to put a band together for Albert. I wasn't 100% sure I wanted to spend a lot of my time on the road gigging when I could be at home writing and spending time with my family, but I knew it had the potential to be a lot of fun and Albert and Irene assured us that we'd be on the road for no longer than three weeks at a time. We managed to get Dave Stewart on drums and Calais Brown on guitar and rehearsals were arranged at Berkeley 2 in Glasgow. We had a couple of days without Albert just to get the songs in shape.

But when Albert arrived and we started rehearsals with him, it became very clear that he was going to be difficult to work with. I didn't get a hard time from him, but some others were really torn to shreds by Albert. It became embarrassing and made everyone feel uncomfortable.

Foss had it particularly bad. Albert didn't like him from day one. He didn't like how Foss interpreted his songs. 'Listen to my records' became his war cry. No one was ever complimented on what they played or what they sang. He'd pick holes in everything, so rehearsals became a nightmare. The songs were very easy to play, partly because they were so melodic and partly because I was already familiar with them. We'd get as far as the first four bars of the first song and Albert stopped and asked Foss what he was playing. He said it was the wrong part and the wrong sound. After the first rehearsal, Albert called me and told me that it wasn't going to work. In my opinion, Foss is an excellent player, especially playing jazz funk. The problem was that Albert needed to hear what was on his records and Foss didn't understand the simplicity of that. Albert wasn't interested in how good Foss was; he just wanted to hear exactly what was on the record being reproduced live. I get that, and I've always understood that he let me get away with improvising, but the keyboards and guitar parts had to be very precise in sound and notation.

Albert was adamant that Foss had to be replaced. It became a struggle and continuing with the rehearsals became embarrassing. Irene called me and said Albert wanted to have dinner to chat about how he wanted things to be and she was with him when I arrived at the restaurant. It was made very clear to me that we had to find another keyboard player ASAP. Kenny Hutchison was the obvious choice as far as I was concerned, as this gig was right up his street. Kenny had played in cover bands often enough to understand how to replicate sounds and parts.

It was obvious from the start that Kenny could handle this gig. Rehearsals went ok, but there was always a bit of tension in the room because you never knew what Albert was going to kick off about next. I began to realise why his Spanish band lost respect for him and why the bass player knocked on his hotel room door and poured a litre of beer over his head. But the gigs were really good and although he gave Kenny and Calais a hard time, he seemed to be very happy with Dave Stewart and myself.

Eventually, Kenny dropped out because of his commitment to teaching music at a Loretto School in Musselburgh. We brought Irvin Duguid onboard and Albert was delighted with him. We also brought in Chrys Lindop for out-front sound; he's a lovely Liverpudlian and a character. The band members and the crew were great; we all got on and had many enjoyable times together. It became a regular event for us to get together for a walk after breakfast and meet in the bar after gigs. Everything was fine, we worked well together and continued with Albert for three years.

Albert had brought a manager on board, an American by the name of David Spiro. We didn't see eye to eye, and I saw him as a passenger, as Albert thought he was going to open up America for him, but it didn't happen. Meanwhile, Spiro was enjoying his business class trips across the Atlantic, classy hotels and free meals, all at Albert's expense. Spiro emailed the band and asked us to take a pay cut for a trip to South Africa.

I believe he was trying to justify his existence as Albert's manager. I said I wouldn't accept a pay cut, so Spiro decided that was a sackable offence. He emailed me and said that Albert and the management wished me luck. They asked if I could recommend anyone to take my place. I suggested Pino Palladino or Tony Levin. Spiro and Albert had no idea who these guys were. So that was it. I was sacked.

Everything fell apart for the Albert Hammond band when they returned from South Africa. Dave and Irvin had had enough and gave Albert and the management a month's notice. It didn't go down well, and there was a lot of bad feeling.

But I had enjoyed the gigs. I enjoyed the places we visited throughout Europe, and Germany in particular. We even played Wuppertal, a place I had been with my family when I was five years old. That was a nostalgic trip. We had our dedicated driver in Lars Bierstroem. Lars lived in the Reeperbahn area of Hamburg, and when we requested a visit to the area that The Beatles frequented, he drove right to the front door of The Kaiserkeller where the Beatles played in the 1960s.

Albert became more and more frustrated with his lack of progress in his endeavours to capture a bigger audience and his grumpiness became more unbearable. Despite that, it was a fantastic three years. There was a lot of fun to be had on days off and the band and crew spent a lot of time together. I discovered a Germany that I never knew existed. I also made a bunch of new friends who looked after each other and made the best of it when times were tough. The compatibility between band, crew and the Hypertension agency made the touring a pure joy, which rarely happens in my experience

2020 to 2022. New projects and old music!

In 2020, Covid 19 raised its ugly head and the UK government announced the first national lockdown on March 23 2020. Many people were hit hard by covid, and we lost friends and family. Musicians were among the people who found that they had no work and venues were closed.

But for those that are creative, work could continue. The brain does not lockdown. Many people were forced to work from home. Musicians could spend their days in the studio working alone, but still working and that is a blessing in these times.

My album *2020* was released on 20th November 2020. It was followed by the single 'No Words', released in February 2021. The song was written during lockdown and reflects the mood and devastating impact the pandemic has had on the planet and its people. Covid 19 mostly affects the respiratory system, including the nose and lungs. When the virus began to take hold and people were admitted to hospital, they were kept in isolation, meaning that relatives were unable to visit and say goodbye to the covid sufferers as they took their last breath.

'No Words'

No more that I can say, no words I can relay
No one wins, when it begins, to take our breath away
No sun to catch my eye, no chance to say goodbye
With a little faith and hope we will survive

Once the vaccines began to be produced and distributed in 2021, we all began to feel some hope, which continues as I complete this book.

In April 2021, the single 'Communication' was released followed by a David Paton and Jon Turner collaboration *I Will Be a King*, which came out in December 2021. Yes, the months I spent during lockdown in the studio have been rewarding, and that is reflected in the amount of work I produced.

At time of writing, we are in the year 2022. The collaboration with Beagle Hat has continued, although the name Beagle Hat was changed (for legal reasons) to Sheep. Our latest collaboration is the 2022 album by David Paton and Sheep, *Melody and Echoes*. This album reached number one in the Japanese Amazon chart, so we now have a happy David Paton and some happy Sheep.

The latest album in 2022 is *The Magic Collection*, and I've released it under the name Pilot. It just seemed like the right album to make. It's no easy task recording music that already has an identity. Reproducing sounds that were recorded almost 50 years ago is a challenge and must be done with precision, expertise and passion.

Many hours were spent working on the Pilot songs to make them sound exciting and contemporary. In some cases, new ideas and arrangements unfolded as the songs began to take shape, adding that extra punch and freshness to the music.

So here I am, flying the flag for Pilot, and I'm excited about this album; I've gone full circle and back to reliving the Pilot music all over again. And Pilot music is very much alive on *The Magic Collection*. It has been a nostalgic trip of pure joy.

2023. Back at Abbey Road

We have already seen that my song 'Magic' has taken on a life of its own.

In 2018 a campaign by the pharmaceutical company Novo Nordisk was launched in the USA for the diabetes drug Ozempic. To spearhead the campaign, they used the song in all their advertisements. I was happy that this allowed it to be heard by a larger audience and it benefitted my CD sales in the USA. On the other hand, I wasn't happy that they'd used session musicians, but as luck would have it, in October of 2022 I received an email from the agency responsible for putting together the advertising campaign. They asked if I was interested in re-recording 'Magic' for a new Ozempic campaign to take place in Summer 2023. Rob Farber was my main point of contact and I also engaged the services of Lisa Moore, a very respected music business lawyer based in Atlanta, Georgia, whom I had used in the past after an introduction from my friend and one-time manager Kirk Kiester. We eventually reached an agreement with Novo Nordisk and Abbey Road was booked for the 18th of February 2023.

The day before the session, Mary and I flew down to Heathrow, where we were picked up by private car and driven to The Covent Garden Hotel. Rob had invited us for dinner that evening, so it was a chance to meet the team and get to know each other a little better in a relaxed way.

We set off from our hotel the following morning, very early. The streets were fairly quiet as we drove along Shaftesbury Avenue and down to Piccadilly. We approached Abbey Road at around 8:30 am and I could see that tourists were already outside the studio and on the famous crossing, taking photos.

As I walked up the steps toward the main door, I was reminded of how many famous musicians had done the same thing. I'd climbed those steps many times and I felt the same level of excitement as if it was the first time. Inside, the reception area was very different; it looked more like a bank with a long counter and security screens. We signed in and walked along to Studio Three. I felt strange, almost as if I were surrounded by ghosts. A flood of distant memories filled my thoughts.

Studio Three itself was totally unrecognisable, as the control room was now where the studio used to be and the studio where the control room was. I'd recorded many albums in Studio Three, including The Alan Parsons Project albums, *Keats* and Pilot's *Two's a Crowd*. I needed a minute to take all this in. The sound guys were busy setting up and there was a lighting crew in the studio unpacking their equipment. Rob started to explain that we'd be working outside with the camera crew for an hour or so, as he wanted video as well as photographs. I was surprised at the scale of the operation; there were a lot of technicians involved.

We made our way outside and walked along the road accompanied by the crew. We had to walk some distance before we found a graffiti-free Abbey Road street sign, but then the photo session began, which caused quite a bit of interest. We spent a while lining up shots and walking through video ideas. Eventually, we moved on to the famous zebra crossing. This also caused a stir as many tourists had already gathered to have their own photos taken there. The shooting began and I found myself pacing back and forward across the road with guitar in hand. Indeed, a number of the video shots required the crew to stand in the middle of the road and stop the traffic. Surprisingly, the London drivers were very patient and seemed to expect this kind of disruption. Finally, we moved on to the steps leading up to the main door of the studio building for a few more photos and videos of me walking into the studios.

It must have taken a couple of hours to complete all the outdoor shots required. Finally, the crew were happy, the Ozempic people were happy and we were all delighted to get back indoors to warm up.

It was now time to move on to recording the vocals. I had already discussed my preferences so the vocal booth was already prepared and the specified microphone I wanted to use (a Neumann U67) was in place. I'd normally do a couple of warm-ups but that was difficult as I felt inhibited by the cameras and lighting which were being set up as I prepared. 'Magic' is not an easy song to sing; it's at the very top of my range, so without a proper warm-up, it took me a few attempts before I was ready to start recording, but I made good progress throughout the various sections of the song.

With a few added backing vocals, the singing was completed within an hour or so and it was time for lunch. We made our way down to the canteen, which created more vivid memories for me. I remembered sitting with Kate Bush and introducing her to my daughter Sara. I also recalled chatting with Paul McCartney when he told me that he played the guitar on 'Taxman'. It was also in that canteen that I was introduced to Eric Woolfson. It was a relief to sit there, eat and relax out of sight of the watchful eye of the camera crew, who seemed to constantly be filming.

Next on the list were guitar overdubs. It is normal to do these in the control room where the producer is close at hand and able to communicate more easily. Greg, the producer, explained that some extra guitar licks would be needed to be played over the edited sections. The commercials would run for 45, 60 or 75 seconds, so smooth edits would need to be created. He played me the edited sections and pointed out where the guitar licks should be. I played a few different ideas that came to mind and he liked what I was playing so we started recording and although the whole process was also filmed, I managed to play without being distracted. I enjoyed interpreting the ideas as they were spontaneous and everything I played seemed to work well, with me using a studio-provided Kemper guitar processor.

Next up on the agenda was the teleprompter. I'd be addressing thousands of Ozempic employees, so even though I had been prepared, it was a daunting task. There were a few paragraphs involved and I needed to look directly into the camera lens and give expression into what I was saying without stumbling. I was surprised that after the first run-through, Rob told me, 'look round, you're getting a standing ovation'. That made me feel a little more confident and I found that I was enjoying it as all the initial fears I had just melted away. Rob sat to the right of the camera and directed me through each stage and eventually, he said, 'that's a wrap, guys'. I joked, 'that's another feather in my cap; musician, songwriter, author and now, actor!'

We finished with an interview. I'm used to those, so this part was relaxed and easy going.

And that was it. Everyone was delighted with the final results and our 12-hour working day ended. A cab was waiting for Mary and me as we left Abbey Road, probably for the last time. But it was a fantastic day and I was happy to be working with such a professional team; everything had gone like clockwork. I felt elated, but also exhausted, slightly numbed, and overjoyed to have been back in the place I had dreamed about visiting when I was 16 years old; the place I eventually worked in for a good 20 years of my career. To say I was emotional about being there again is a bit of an understatement, and I am grateful to Ozempic for using my song and allowing the day to happen.

Thanks to Rob, Greg, Jenn and all of the team for making the day very special; it really was, a bit of 'Magic'.

Epilogue

Time is marching on; a lot can happen in a year. I began writing my memoirs so that my grandkids Jackson, Ava and Jamie and great-grandkids (yet to arrive) could have an insight into the life I had as a musician. I started writing about the people I had met in my career as a musician, but it evolved into a bigger picture that includes family, health, and general life experiences. I have read through what I have written and now I see it as a bit of a life story. I can see how things developed and reached a pinnacle. I know that the best years of my career are behind me and I have managed to move on to a more relaxed way of living. Letting go of the past is just as important as embracing the future but what is most important for me is now. We live our lives and make the most of what we enjoy and endure. The majority of us can cope and proceed through life accepting that this is how it is, and that this is what has been given to us. In a lot of cases, life seems to be very unfair. Positivity and optimism have played a part in the way things are for me. Knowing when a stage in life has run its course and moving on is also important. I have managed to relive a lot of the experiences I went through, and that's mainly because I wrote them down here. I know that living in the past is not a good place to be, but a little glimpse seems to be OK sometimes.

I can now put my memoirs behind me and look upon this book as an achievement and an insight into my life.

And that is what it is.

Left: Mary at Blarney Castle, Ireland, in 2018. (*David Paton Collection*)

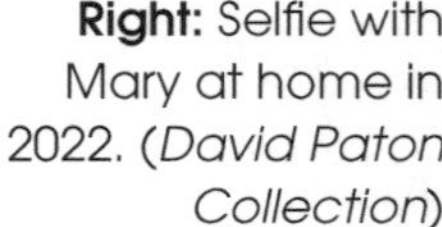

Right: Selfie with Mary at home in 2022. (*David Paton Collection*)

Right: Jackson and Ava on space hoppers! (*David Paton Collection*)

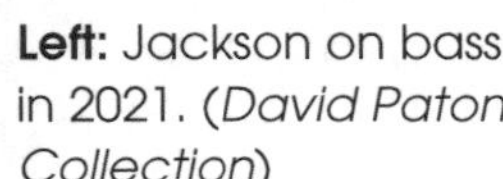

Left: Jackson on bass in 2021. (*David Paton Collection*)

Above: My daughters Katy and Sarah in 2014. (*Stuart Stott*)

Right: Jackson and Sarah.(*David Paton Collection*)

Appendix. David Paton Discography

1968	Single	Boots	The Animal in Me
1968	Single	Boots	Keep Your Lovelight Burning
1971	Single	Christyan	Nursery Lane
1973	Album	The Loreburn Singers	Bless this House
1974	Album	Pilot	From The Album of The Same Name
1974	Single	Scotch Mist	Ra Ta Ta
1975	Album	Pilot	Second Flight
1975	Single	Jack Harris	Sail Away
1975	Single	Pilot	Lady Luck
1975	Album	David Courtney	First Day
1976	Album	The Alan Parsons Project	Tales of Mystery & Imagination
1976	Album	Pilot	Morin Heights
1976	Album	William Lyall	Solo Casting
1976	Single	Marylin Miller	You've Got to Get Me Higher
1977	Album	Pilot	Two's a Crowd
1977	Album	The Alan Parsons Project	I Robot
1977	Single	Paul McCartney & Wings	Mull of Kintyre
1978	Album	The Alan Parsons Project	Pyramid
1978	Album	Don Black & Geoff Stephens	Dear Anyone
1978	Album	Kate Bush	The Kick Inside
1978	Album	Kate Bush	Lionheart
1979	Album	The Alan Parsons Project	Eve
1979	Album	Chris De Burgh	Crusader
1980	Album	The Alan Parsons Project	The Turn of a Friendly Card
1980	Album	Pilot	The Best of Pilot
1981	Album	Chris Rea	Chris Rea
1981	Album	Elaine Paige	Elaine Paige
1981	Album	John Townley	More Than a Dream
1982	Album	The Alan Parsons Project	Eye in the Sky
1982	Album	Jimmy Page	Death Wish II (III) OST
1982	Album	Camel	Single Factor
1983	Album	The Alan Parsons Project	The Best of The Alan Parsons Project
1983	Album	Andrew Powell + The Philharmonia Orchestra	Plays the Best of The APP
1984	Album	The Alan Parsons Project	Ammonia Avenue
1984	Album	The Alan Parsons Project	Vulture Culture
1984	Album	Camel	Stationary Traveller

1984	Album	Keats	Keats
1985	Album	The Alan Parsons Project	Stereotomy
1985	Album	Elton John	Ice on Fire
1985	Album	Original Motion Pic. S/T	Ladyhawke
1985	Album	Various Artists	Performance The Best of Tim Rice & Andrew Lloyd Webber
1986	Album	Elton John	Leather Jackets
1987	Album	Elton John	Live in Australia
1987	Album	The Alan Parsons Project	Tales of Mystery & Imagination 87
1987	Album	The Alan Parsons Project	Best of Volume 2
1988	Album	The Alan Parsons Project	The Instrumental Works
1988	Album	Elton John	Reg Strikes Back
1988	Single	Silvia Griffin	Love's a State of Mind
1988	Album	Rick Wakeman	Time Machine
1988	Album	Rick Wakeman	The Word & The Gospels
1989	Album	The Alan Parsons Project	Pop Classics (Compilation)
1989	Album	Matia Bazar	Red Corner
1989	Album	Frank Ryan	You You
1989	Album	Aleksander Mezek	Podarjeno Srcu
1990	Album	Caterina Caselli	Amada Mia
1990	Album	Propaganda1234	
1990	Album	Ron	Apri Le Braccia E Poi Vola
1991	Album	Rick Wakeman	The Classical Connection
1991	Album	Rick Wakeman	The Classical Connection 2
1991	Album	Rick Wakeman	The New Gospels
1991	Album	Rick Wakeman	Softsword
1991	Album	Camel	Dust & Dreams
1991	Album	The Alan Parsons Project	Prime Time: The Alan Parsons Project Best
1991	Album	The Alan Parsons Project	Anthology (Connoisseur Collection)
1991	Album	Fish	Internal Exile
1991	Album	Davie Paton	Passions Cry
1991	Album	Richard Thompson	Sweet Talker
1992	Album	The Alan Parsons Project	Anthology (Italy)
1992	Album	The Alan Parsons Project	Hits in the Sky (Hong Kong)
1992	Album	The Alan Parsons Project	The Best of the Alan Parsons Project (France)

1992	Album	The Alan Parsons Project	The Ultimate Collection
1992	Album	Fish	Derek Dick & His Amazing Electric Bear
1992	Album	Fish	For Whom the Bell Tolls
1992	Album	Fish	There's a Guy Works Down the Chip Shop...
1992	Album	Fish	Toiling in the Reeperbahn
1992	Album	Fish	Uncle Fish & The Crypt Creepers
1992	Album	The River Detectives	Elvis Has Left the Building
1993	Album	The Pretenders	The Last of the Independents
1993	Album	Rick Wakeman	Prayers
1993	Album	Fish	Songs From the Mirror
1993	Album	Fish/Various Artists	Outpatients 93
1994	Album	Fish	Sushi
1994	Album	Fish	Suits
1994	Single	Fish	Lady Let it Lie
1994	Album	Fish	Lucky Bastards
1994	Album	Fish	Fortunes of War
1994	Album	Rick Wakeman	Almost Live in Europe
1994	Album	Camel	On the Road 1982
1995	Album	Fish	Acoustic Sessions
1995	Album	Fish	Yin
1995	Album	Fish	Yang
1995	Album	Fiona Kennedy	Maiden Heaven
1996	Album	Blair Douglas	A Summer in Skye
1996	Album	Rick Wakeman	Orisons
1996	Album	Rick Wakeman	Can You Hear Me
1996	Album	Camel	Harbour of Tears
1996	Album	Davie Paton	Fragments
1997	Album	Gerry O' Beirne	Half Moon Bay
1997	Album	The Alan Parsons Project	Gold Collection
1997	Album	The Alan Parsons Project	The Definitive Collection
1997	Album	Connie Dover	If I Ever Return
1997	Album	Andy M. Stewart	Donegal Rain
1998	Album	Fish	Kettle of Fish
1998	Album	John McNairn	Borderland
1998	Album	Alexander Mezek	Presented to the Heart
1998	Album	Dick Gaughan	Redwood Cathedral
1999	Album	The Alan Parsons Project	36 All-Time Greatest Hits

1999	Album	The Alan Parsons Project	Eye in the Sky: The Encore Collection
1999	Album	The Alan Parsons Project	Master Hits: The Heritage Series
1999	Album	Tannas	Suileandubh (Dark Eyes)
1999	Album	Margaret Callan	Faileasan Uibhist
1999	Single	Donnie Munro with Holly Thomas	Will You Walk on By
1999	Album	Fish	The Complete BBC Sessions
2000	Album	McAllias	Highwired
2000	Album	Donnie Munro	Donnie Munro
2001	Album	V.A. (Tribute to Kevin Wilkinson)	Green Indians
2002	Album	V.A. The Music of Marc Bolan & T Rex	Legacy
2002	Album	Kenny Herbert	The Last Song in Abbey Road
2002	Single	Kenny Herbert	A Man's a Man for A' That
2002	Single	Kenny Herbert	Live The Life
2002	Single	Kenny Herbert	Money Tree Fun
2002	Single	Kenny Herbert	Ever Changing Times
2002	Single	Kenny Herbert	I Can't Imagine Christmas Without You
2002	Album	Donnie Munro	Across the City and the World
2002	Single	Donnie Munro	She Knows Love
2002	Single	Donnie Munro	The Weaver of Grass
2002	Album	Holly Thomas	Oubliette
2002	Album	Pilot	Blue Yonder
2003	Album	Nobby Clark	If Only
2003	Album	David Paton	The Search
2003	Album	Ray Wilson	Change
2005	Album	Nobby Clark	Going Home
2006	Album	Beagle Hat	Magical Hat
2006	Album	Kenny Herbert	Songs of our Lives
2007	Album	David Paton	Fellow man
2007	Album	David Paton & friends	Originals
2007	Album	Pilot	Craighall Demos
2008	Album	Nobby Clark	On the Inside
2008	Album	Archie Fisher	Windward away
2009	Album	Eric Woolfson	Eric Woolfson sings The Alan Parsons Project that never was

2009	Album	Beagle Hat	Orange Groove
2010	Album	David Paton	Under the sun
2010	Album	Rococo	Run from the Wildfire
2012	Album	X11 Alfonso	Charles Darwin
2013	Album	Sarastro Blake	New Progmantics
2014	Album	Pilot	A Pilot Project
2015	Album	Jules Knight	Change of Heart
2019	Single	Rooftop Screamers	Your day will Come
2019	Album	David Paton	The Traveller
2020	Album	Louise Rutkowski	Dear Boy
2020	Album	David Paton	2020
2021	Single	David Paton	No Words
2021	Single	David Paton	Communication
2021	Single	David Paton & Jon Turner	I will be a King
2022	Album	David Paton & Sheep	Melody and Echoes
2022	Album	Pilot	The Magic Collection

Mary and I in Ireland. (*David Paton Collection*)